# THE BIBLICAL DOCTRINE
# OF THE CHURCH

*The*

# BIBLICAL

# DOCTRINE

*of the*

# CHURCH

By

WILLIAM ROBINSON, M.A., D.D., S.T.D.

*Professor of Christian Doctrine and the Philosophy of Religion,
Selly Oak Colleges, Birmingham, England; and
Principal, Overdale College*

*Reproduced by permission of*
Chalice Press

**Wipf and Stock Publishers**
*150 West Broadway • Eugene OR 97401*

The Biblical Doctrine of the Church
by William Robinson
Copyright©1948 by C. D. Pantle

ISBN: 0-9653517-7-7

Printed by *Wipf and Stock Publishers*
150 West Broadway • Eugene OR 97401

*Printed in the United States of America*

# FOREWORD

THIS book is the result of an invitation from the dean and faculty of the School of Religion, Butler University, Indianapolis, to deliver a course of eight lectures in that institution during the period of September 11-17, 1947. It came at a time when I had been considering the possibility of writing on "The Biblical Doctrine of the Church" and gave me the opportunity to formulate my thoughts. The eight lectures are printed as delivered; the Appendixes have been added to make the biblical survey more complete.

In Chapters I, III, V, VI, and VII, I have used material which was originally prepared for the Commission of the Edinburgh Conference, 1937, which dealt with "The Church and the Word of God," and which published the book, *Die Kirche Jesu Christi und das Wort Gottes*. The book does not attempt to deal with the question of the sacraments or, strictly speaking, with the question of the ministry. Lausanne (1927) dealt exhaustively with these questions, and it was then clear to me that no progress could be made until the subject of the nature of the church was tackled. Unfortunately, Edinburgh, ten years later, went over much the same ground as did Lausanne.

It then became obvious that little further progress could be made toward understanding the ministry and sacraments until both Protestants and Catholics had come to an understanding of what is meant by "the church." They were often speaking different languages. At Edinburgh it was decided to make the doctrine of the church a major study for the next meeting, and a commission was appointed to deal with the subject. In dealing with the church as an ongoing institution in history, it has been necessary to touch upon the structure of the church and in the last two chapters to say something on the subject of apostolic succession, which is the major point of separation between the Protestant and Catholic conceptions of the church. These two chapters have necessarily had to be more controversial, and more given to quotation, but I have tried to maintain the irenic spirit and hope that I have succeeded to some extent.

The lectures were mainly addressed to a Disciple (Churches of Christ) audience, which explains certain references to the writings of Alexander Campbell and other prominent leaders in the movement which brought the Disciple communion into being. These early Disciple doctors and teachers will be unfamiliar to those unacquainted with our tradition, partly owing to the fact that in the second and succeeding generations of our history we had, due to a failure to understand some of the major emphases of this early teaching, shut ourselves in and stood apart from the rest of the Christian world. To anyone familiar with the writings of Alexander Campbell, it ought not to be a matter of surprise that one reared in that tradition should give himself to a study of the doctrine of the church, for that was a major concern of early Disciple teachers. The first proposition of the *Declaration and Address*, issued in 1809 by Thomas Campbell, was "That the church of Christ upon earth is essentially, intentionally, and constitutionally one." The main interest was in the *visible* church, and the sole purpose was that the scattered forces of Christianity might be gathered into "one holy catholic apostolic church." Schism, wherever it existed, was sin: "There ought to be no schisms, nor uncharitable division." This document was almost a century before its time. In a sense, it was a Catholic voice speaking from the Protestant fold. Unfortunately, at the time it appeared, it could result in no other issue than the setting up of one more church within the already divided Christian community, for the Campbells and their followers were driven out of the Presbyterian fold and later out of the Baptist fold, where they had sought refuge. The interest in the doctrine of the church and the passion for the unity of Christians in the one church was, however, never completely lost

[ 7 ]

by those who followed them "without the camp." This book, I hope, will serve to make their memory green to many of these same followers in the present day and bring them to the notice of many for whom they are not even a name.

WILLIAM ROBINSON.

*Overdale College,*
*Selly Oak,*
*Birmingham, England*
*Spring, 1948*

# ACKNOWLEDGMENTS

IT WAS indeed a great honor to be asked to deliver this series of lectures in a university which, though young in comparsion with some of the more hoary foundations in Europe, is so justly famous for its scholarship and learning, not only here but in my own country as well. Ever since I was a young man, eager to pursue the path of knowledge, though, as becomes a young man, not unduly burdened with the weight of learning, I have been proud of Butler University. As a student in seminary work in the ancient University of Oxford, fair mother of our English universities, not excepting Cambridge, it was a proud moment of my life to discover in the University Statutes that Butler, along with Yale and Harvard, was a recognized university on this continent. In more recent years, this School of Religion has been made famous by having as its head, for so many years, Dean Frederick D. Kershner, whom I am proud to number among my friends. Today, with a leading economist, such as President Ross, as the head of the university, and with Dr. Shelton, whose abilities daily become more apparent, as the dean of the School of Religion, the future of both university and school is secure.

I cannot forget the kindness shown to my wife and myself during our stay at Butler, both by Dr. and Mrs. Shelton and by members of the faculty—kindness doubly appreciated after the barren wastes of eight years of rationing in England.

The School of Religion has had many distinguished guests in past years, including the late William Temple, Archbishop of Canterbury, William E. Hocking, and Reinhold Niebuhr—men whose standards I cannot hope to reach but in whose footsteps I may humbly follow and hope that my own will not be too faltering. Never in my wildest dreams did I contemplate being called to this task, and I am deeply sensitive of the honor that was paid me. My country is deeply indebted to America, both for friendship and generosity. The traffic known as "Lend-lease" is familiar to us all. I can only hope that in sharing my deepest thoughts on the subject of the church, I may be able to make some slight return for the many kindnesses and courtesies which America has shown to Britain in these past troubled years.

To the following owners of copyrighted materials quoted herein, grateful acknowledgment is made: the Clarendon Press, Oxford, for permission to quote from Robert Bridges' *The Testament of Beauty;* Professor C. H. Dodd and the Cambridge University Press and the Macmillan Company, New York, for permission to quote from *The Bible To-Day*; Professor C. H. Dodd and Hodder and Stoughton and Harper and Brothers, New York, for permission to quote from *The Moffat Commentary on the Johannine Epistles*; Mr. T. J. Cadoux and the Lutterworth Press for permission to quote from Dr. C. J. Cadoux's *The Historic Mission of Jesus*; Canon W. J. Phythian-Adams and the Student Christian Movement Press for permission to quote from *The Way of At-one-ment*; the Student Christian Movement Press for permission to quote from my chapter in *Ministry and Sacraments*; the Macmillan Company, London, for permission to quote from William Temple's *Thoughts on Some Problems of the Day*; and the editor of the *Hibbert Journal* and Allen and Unwin for permission to use parts of two articles of mine in the issues for April, 1941, and April, 1943.

W. R.

# CONTENTS

# I

## THE COMING OF THE CHURCH

THE necessity and nature of the church are grounded in the fact and character of revelation. This means that any division, such as is common in our day, between the word of God and the church is a division which belongs to the realm of the abstract, rather than to that of reality. Such a division is completely foreign to the Bible, both Old and New Testaments. In the Bible it is just as foreign to ask whether a man can be a Christian without being a member of the Christian church as it is to ask whether a man can be a Jew without belonging to the Israel of God. This is so because the church is the *fellowship* (*koinōnia*), and the whole work of creation and redemption— God's activity on and within the historical plane—is just God's bid for fellowship with man.[1] And this creative and redemptive activity of God is what the Bible means by "revelation" (Heb. *gālāh*; Gr. *apocalypsis*).[2]

It has been our interpretation of the doctrines of creation and redemption in mechanical or legal (transactional) terms, rather than in *personal* terms, which has blinded us to this truth. We have been all too

[ 15 ]

ready to conceive of God's relationship to the world and to history as mechanical and legal, rather than as personal. In mechanical and legal relationships the narrower logic of the schools always holds good, and so we have produced our completely rational theologies. But in personal relationships this narrower logic is never adequate. In this realm a higher form of reason than logic holds good, for—

>'tis mightily
>to the reproach of Reason that she cannot save
>nor guide the herd.*

It was at this higher realm that even a rational theologian like Anselm hinted when writing of the sublime mysteries of the Incarnation and the atonement.[3] He was not unaware, as he tells us, of the higher reasons of the spirit, and he did not really believe that—

>the embranglements
>of logic wer the prime condition of all Being,
>the essence of things.†

His rational theology was nothing more than a methodology suited to the times. All such completely merely rational theologies are subpersonal; for there

---

*Robert Bridges, *The Testament of Beauty*, Book I, lines 609-11. Used by permission of the Clarendon Press, Oxford.

†Bridges, *op. cit.*, lines 432-34. Used by permission.

is that in personality which is suprarational—a subtle
essence which cannot be captured or confined, though
it may be "caught." Personality is the real miracle of
the universe. It is not a mathematical entity, subject
to the laws of subtraction and addition. One and one
do not make two in the realm of personality:

> And I know not if, save in this, such gift be allowed to man,
>> That out of three sounds he frame, not a fourth sound,
>>> but a star.[4]

For beyond personality is suprapersonality, which is
*fellowship*, the most potent thing in the world—the
interpenetration of personality, or the sharing of personality without its loss: "This Individualism is
man's true Socialism."[5]

Such fellowship is a complete contradiction of all
forms of pantheistic mysticism,[6] which teach the absorption of the individual in the World-soul and talk
of—

> A shoreless, soundless sea,
> Wherein at last our souls must fall.[7]

Such a mysticism is foreign to the biblical revelation,
where individual personality is treated with respect
and with reverence, but where the solitary person,
out of fellowship with God and with his fellow
man, is regarded as a defective personality. All this,

in the end, means that God himself is not unitary but manifold, a truth which is adequately safeguarded, though not completely defined, in the Christian doctrine of the Sacred Trinity.[8] Further, it implies that the whole meaning of creation and redemption—of Providence—is to be found in God's bid for fellowship; for fellowship is the hidden structure of reality.

The ground of this assertion that *fellowship* is the essential nature of reality—what we would see if only our eyes were open to the spiritual nature of things—is not based on philosophical speculation, but is *given* to us in *revelation*, the self-disclosure of God himself. Revelation, in the biblical sense, is the unfolding of the "hidden secret" through the gracious activity of God—something *done* in the realm of *fact*, something *objectively* set forth, a sure word of God. In nature, God is not necessarily seen as personal, nor is the world seen as ordered fellowship. The secret is never wholly revealed. In revelation, however—in the word of God in its manifoldness, first acted and spoken and finally "made flesh"—the truth that fellowship is the structure of reality is completely set forth. This difference between God as revealed in nature and God as revealed in history, in the Word of God, is the whole difference between pantheism and pantheistic mysticisms (nonpersonal mysticisms) on the one hand and Christianity on the other.[9] In another sense, it constitutes the difference between all types of deistic transcendence on the one hand and Christianity on the other.

This is the point, it seems to me, which is being made by the writer of the prologue of the Fourth Gospel. He is writing about revelation—the manifestation or showing forth (epiphany) of the nature and character of God on the plane of history. In so writing, he has in mind two types of religion which, in the missionary sphere, were in his day, and still are in other forms, rivals of Christianity. First, he has in mind Judaism, which had rejected Christ and which, in his scheme, stands for deistic transcendence—a one-way movement—the movement from God to us. Secondly, he has in mind certain types of what we should call theosophy or anthroposophy, which can be characterized as "flights from reality"—attempts to escape from the real concreteness of things and events. And these again express a one-way movement—the movement from us to God—the "upward lift" of all humanisms and subjectivisms. Over against these, he sets the doctrine of the Word of God, who was with God and who was God (the paradox of immanence and transcendence), the Word of God who *comes* and *is received*. Here, in contrast, is a double movement, the movement from God to us and back from us to God, involving the paradox of transcendence and immanence, but immanence of a personalistic and concrete type.[10] In the prologue, this movement from God to us and from us to God—this process, or better still, this series of acts of revelation—is set forth as finally assuming incarnational form. Further, it is set forth as a threefold movement, deepening in intensity and increasing in concreteness, and becoming more vivid in its objectivity.

After the introduction in verses 1-5 and an aside in verses 6-8, which need not concern us here, we have the *first movement* in verses 9 and 10: "The true light that enlightens every man was coming into the world; he was in the world, and the world was made through him, yet the world knew him not." This I take to be the most widely diffused activity of the Word in the prehistory of the world, before the choice of any special "Israel of God" (any church). It represents a stage in the creative and redemptive activity of God in which he is in the world, but the world knows him not. We must further remember that the writer of this Gospel uses the word "know" of that kind of knowledge which is concrete and personal, rather than discursive and abstract; that kind of knowledge which, for want of a better word, we call "intuitive" and which has about it the quality of givenness. That kind of knowledge, which is what fellowship is built upon, was not present at this stage. In the Bible, "knowing God" means knowing the *living* God. It has little to do with metaphysical knowledge of God and is almost wholly concerned with knowledge of his *character* and *purpose*.[11]

The *second movement* is set forth in verses 11-13: "He came to his own home and his own people received him not. But to all who received him, who believed in his name, he gave power to become children of God; who were born, not of blood nor of the will of the flesh nor of the will of man, but of God." It is really two movements in one, but two movements which have the same incarnational quality, merely differing in intensity. Surely, in these verses the writer has in mind, not the Incarnation proper, but the choice of Abraham and his seed. This is the movement of God in history which began when Abraham "went out, not knowing where he was to go"—Abraham the man of faith. At that moment the church of God— God's holy Israel—came into being. Here is the process of selectivity beginning in crisis, the process which involves "covenant";[12] not the smooth movement upward of the older evolutionary view of history, but the "striking down" of God, a declaration of an "eternal now" in the time process. Here the church comes into being. Abraham and his seed were chosen to a missionary vocation in the world. In the main they rejected God, they "received him not." The Old Testament is the story of a people chosen to a missionary vocation who mistook responsibility for privilege, who rejected every prophet, lawgiver, psalmist, and apocalyptist who ever voiced this vocation and finally slew the only Son of their race who perfectly fulfilled it and embodied it in his own life.

So, within the "Israel of God," there had to be further selectivity, the setting apart of the "true Israel" (or the "remnant" or "little flock") as over against the "false Israel." These were they who "received him" (the Word), who met the eternal "yea" with an affirmation. They were the "servants" or "sons of God"—

> Souls temper'd with fire,
> Fervent, heroic, and good,
> Helpers and friends of mankind.
>
> Servants of God!—or sons
> Shall I not call you? because
> Not as servants ye knew
> Your Father's innermost mind.[13]

Here, I take it, the prologue refers to the prophets, priests, psalmists, sages, and apocalyptists, who, although they had often been down in the valley, where there were all kinds of crudities and failures of vision, and where it was not always possible to see clearly and rarely very far, had not only caught glimpses of the heights above, but had even been translated to those heights and, in a transfigured moment, had gained a vision, clear and far and wide, of things *sub specie aeternitatis*. It should be carefully noted that this "true Israel" was not a fleshly Israel. These "sons of God" had a spiritual birth—they "were born of God." The quality which constituted them the "true Israel" was not a quality of race, but a moral and spiritual one. Here the veil is beginning to be rent, and we are able to see something of the true nature of fellowship as it is in God and as it must be on earth.

The *third movement* is set forth in verse 14: "And the Word became flesh and dwelt among us [tabernacled with us][14] full of grace and truth; and we beheld his glory, glory as of the only Son from the Father." This, I take it, refers to the Incarnation proper—the revelation of the Word in Jesus Christ our Lord—a revelation so concrete that the Word becomes manifested (placarded on the plane of history) in a purely local and temporal form and in a concrete living personality. Here we reach a limiting point of concretion in the process; we see shown forth what we might call "the concretion of the Absolute."

In all this it is clear that the word of God has never been a purely *verbal* word. It has been given in *act* rather than in *phrase*. It is neither an ideology nor a set of ideologies; neither a law nor a set of laws involving a legal system of ethical and ceremonial rightness; not something marked by logical consistency; but something "full of grace and truth," a living reality and a compelling certainty within a given set of existents, so that our faith in it is not dependent upon anything so subjective as value judgments but upon judgments of existence.

This, of course, means that revelation is never infallible in the sense in which it has been conceived to be in traditional theories of inspiration in both Catholic and Protestant systems though it is infallible in a deeper sense. Man's search for an infallibility of the rigid, verbal, and legal type is a vain one. An infallible declaration of this kind would need an infallible mind to understand it and interpret it. But an infallible mind is just the kind of mind which would have no need for such a declaration. The whole thing is a delusion and ought to worry us no longer. Both Judaism and Christianity are agreed that in the end, in the absolute, God's ways are past finding out; but they both rely fully on the guidance of God in history, that is, on revelation. The older view may be regarded as a theory of "infallibility without limits." Such a theory belongs to those systems which may be regarded as "flights from reality," and both Judaism and Christianity are far too closely wedded to history—to what is actual—to find room for such theories. It is true that both Jewish and Christian Scholastic systems have propounded theories of "infallibility without limits," but such theories are alien to the temper of both religions, and, paradoxically enough, they have been found to carry with them nothing but limits—they have been the means of binding and not of loosing. But neither can Judaism nor Christianity be satisfied with theories which equate revelation with discovery, which so reduce everything to subjectivity that there is no givenness; for a religion which has nothing to give to the world, except what it takes out of the world, has nothing to give and is no religion at all. It is when we realize that revelation is divinely contrived but humanly conditioned, that our limits set a limit on God in the sense in which he may be fulfilled in us, that we do not rob ourselves of the idea of infallibility but arrive at a notion of infallibility which is existential and concrete. This, if we like to call it so, may be described as "infallibility with limits," and it is just this kind of infallibility, paradoxically enough, which carries with it no limits.

[ 25 ]

For this reason it can never be completely conveyed in *verbal* form. At its highest it has for its vehicle the "divine act." It is perhaps better described as "infallibility of act," for action is final in a sense in which the spoken word can never be, as Alexander Campbell pointed out a century ago in his *Christian System*, as did Walter Scott in his *The Messiahship*. Origen had become aware early in the third century, through his study of the Fourth Gospel, of the need of a somewhat similar theory of revelation. He declares that it was the purpose of the Evangelist "to give the truth, where possible, at once spiritually and corporeally, but where this was not possible, to prefer the spiritual to the corporeal, the true spiritual meaning being often preserved, as one might say, in the corporeal falsehood" (*Commentary on St. John's Gospel*, x. 4). But the words of the younger Isaac Penington, in the seventeenth century, are perhaps more to the point: "All truth is a shadow except the last. But every truth is substance in its own place, though it be but a shadow in another place. And the shadow is a true shadow, as the substance is a true substance."[15]

We do not get beyond history and reach out into the eternal by regarding the historical as the insecure element in religion and seeking to build on some necessity unrelated to the time process, and therefore to what seems relative and evanescent. This path does not lead us to some objective standard unaffected by time and change. Such an attempt to ignore history can never achieve the result it sets out to achieve, for it reduces us to relying on judgments of value over against judgments of existence, and all such reliance is mere subjectivism, the creation of religion for ourselves. We can only reach out beyond history if God has entered into history, which means that we must take history seriously and give a proper place to judgments of existence. It is when we "take history seriously that we shall find that we cannot regard religion as projection or illusion."[16]

It is, therefore, within the concrete living personality of Jesus of Nazareth, the Word made flesh, that we most clearly see God making his bid for fellowship. The first thing that strikes us about the teaching of Jesus is that it is, on his own claims, a reflection into human life of the mind and spirit of God. If we ask why men should order their lives and their relations to other men by what appears to be such a topsy-turvy system of ethics, the answer is, Because the nature of God is such.[17] It is, therefore, most important for human living that we should have a right conception of God, not in the narrower sense of the creeds, but in the sense of keeping ourselves from idols. For

Jesus, God was personal—our Father—and the whole business of producing an ordered world was the business of creating fellowship, which is the highest destiny of personality and its only hope of salvation.

There is, of course, a realm of God's impersonal dealing, but it is not the realm in which religion and morality are to function. When religion enters this realm it degenerates into magic, and when morality concerns itself with it, it "goes west" and ceases to exist. This is the realm in which many religious people have tried to "force the hand of God," have been over-anxious to push open doors which God has not opened. But Jesus taught us not to draw hasty conclusions from towers falling on people and from wholesale murders by tyrants. True religion finds its home in the realm of God's *personal* dealing with men and women, and a true social order can never be reared except upon the foundation of this incontrovertible fact and on the fact that *personality*, therefore, is of inestimable worth.

When we look at revelation in this way, in its relationship to history, and, so far as the Christian revelation is concerned, its relationship to a "history within history," to a "holy history," we see that the Bible "depicts God's ways with man in the 'large letters' of the history of community."[18] It is a book about the church and only about the individual as he is related to the community. The Old Testament has no meaning apart from the solidarity of the nation, the "people of God," and this is just as much true of the prophetic understanding as it is of the Torah, as true of the later prophets, who understand individual responsibility, as of the earlier prophets. In Exodus it is said, "Israel is my son, my first-born" (4:22); in Hosea, "Israel is a luxuriant vine" (10:1); in Jeremiah, "My people have been lost sheep" (50:6); and in Ezekiel, "Now will I bring back the captivity of Jacob, and have mercy upon the whole house of Israel" (39:25). Such passages could be multiplied. There is no understanding of the Bible apart from what Wheeler Robinson has called "the idea of corporate personality."

The biography of a people is told as though it were the biography of an individual, as in the beautiful poem of the eleventh chapter of Hosea, or as in many parts of Deuteronomy: "And thou shalt remember all the ways which the LORD thy God hath led thee these forty years in the wilderness, that he might humble thee, to prove thee, to know what was in thy heart. . . . Thy raiment waxed not old upon thee, neither did thy foot swell, these forty years." (Deut. 8:2-4.) Not even the most individualistic prophet ever conceived himself as being outside the Israel of God, nor were the prophets so conceived to be by what might be called the ecclesiastics of the postexilic period, or their books would not have been included in the Canon. They would have gone down into oblivion, and we should never have heard of them. The covenant of God is a covenant with a people and not with an individual. This is as true of the "new covenant" which Jeremiah sees as it is of the "old covenant": "Behold the days come, saith the LORD, that I will make a new covenant *with the house of Israel, and with the house of Judah:* not according to the covenant that I made with their fathers in the day that I took them by the  hand to bring them out of the land of Egypt; which my covenant they brake, although I was a husband unto them, saith the LORD. But this is the covenant which I will make *with the house of Israel* after those days, saith the LORD: I will put my law in their inward parts, and in their hearts will I write it; and I will be their God, and *they shall be my people.*" (31:31-33.)  Whatever is said about individual knowledge of God, there is no idea here of the individual apart from his relationship to the community.

The same sense of corporeity is seen in the idea of Israel as the bride of Yahweh, which appears in Hosea, Jeremiah, and Second Isaiah,[19] and again in the idea of Israel as the vine of David.[20]  Within this corporate sense there emerges the idea of the "true

[ 30 ]

Israel" over against the "false Israel," but the "true Israel" is a corporate conception. There is no possibility of being in a right relation to God without being in relationship to one's fellow man. This notion of the "true Israel," or "remnant," becomes important from the time of the Exile onward, though it is there in Jeremiah and in Isaiah before the Exile.[21] Indeed it forms the main theme of two chapters which scholars are more and more inclined to ascribe to Isaiah proper (chaps. 10 and 11). In Second Isaiah it is linked with the "suffering servant of Yahweh," an idea which is now recognized by scholars to be corporate: "But thou, Israel, my servant, Jacob whom I have chosen, the seed of Abraham my friend" (41:8). In what have been called "the servant songs" it is clear that in some cases, as in the passage just quoted, "the servant" is the whole of Israel; in others, he appears to be "Israel within Israel," "the remnant"; and finally, he is one single son of Israel in whom the whole of Israel is embodied, a corporate personality. This is clearest in Isaiah 42:1-4, where "the servant" is called God's "elect," another important expression, and in the best known of "the servant songs," Isaiah 52:13-53:12, the one which played such an important part in the pre-Pauline church's understanding of the life and death of our Lord. It is important to remember in this connection that in the primitive church's under-

standing of our Lord, Jesus is not only the long promised deliverer, God's Messiah to Israel, not only the
Son of God in the Messianic and in the Pauline sense
of the pre-existent Son; but he is also, together with
those who are "with him," the "Israel of God," God's
"elect," and finally, on the cross, the "Israel of God
reduced to one Man."

There is still further that strange apocalyptic expression, the "Son of man," which plays such an important part in the Gospels, and which is there applied by Jesus to himself, certainly after the confession
at Caesarea Philippi, if not before. It appears first in
Ezekiel, though perhaps not in the technical sense
which it later acquires. In Daniel 7:13-14 it has
this technical sense: "Behold, one like the Son of
man came with the clouds of heaven, and came to
the Ancient of days. . . . And there was given him
dominion, and glory, and a kingdom, that all people,
nations, and languages, should serve him: his dominion is an everlasting dominion" (A.V.). In the
apocalyptic literature, much of it written in the two
centuries preceding the Christian Era, the term
plays a most important part, and this explains its appearance in the Gospels. Professor J. R. Coates and,
later, Professor T. W. Manson have argued convinc-
ingly that this, too, is a corporate expression, parallel
to the "Israel of God," and the "suffering servant"

and narrowing in content until one Man in Israel is identified with the Son of man.[22] They have argued that the expression, as used by Jesus in the Synoptic Gospels, includes with himself those who are "with him," until at last in the death, burial, and resurrection, he stands alone as the Son of man. Not until his coming, is the perfect Israel of God, the perfect church, revealed.

In the light of all this, we may sum up with some words of Professor C. H. Dodd:

> The history of the Old Testament consists of alternating phases of crisis and development through which Israel is shaped, under the divine providence, into a people of God. All through, but notably in the latest phase, there is a sense of inconclusiveness and a forward reference. Always Israel is the people of God, and at the same time is *not yet* the people of God in the fullest sense. The ideal attributes which the prophets applied to Israel are finally understood to await realization in an age yet to come, when God will intervene with a mighty hand to fulfill his purpose.*

Professor Dodd then notes how the New Testament writers take up these ideal attributes and apply them to the church. In Galatians, the church is the "Israel of God" (6:16). In 1 Peter, it is "God's own people" (2:9), whose members are a kingdom of priests to God (Rev. 1:6). To Paul, it is Isaiah's

---

*The Bible To-day, p. 70. Used by permission of the Cambridge University Press, the Macmillan Co., and Professor Dodd.

righteous remnant (Rom. 9:27), Jeremiah's people of the new covenant (2 Cor. 3:5f.), Daniel's saints of the Most High (1 Cor. 1:2). "This is not enthusiastic rhetoric," declares Professor Dodd. "It is deliberate reapplication of prophetic language. It amounts to an assertation that the people of God has now passed through its supreme crisis, and reached its complete and final form."[23] No longer is the church coming; it has come. The "Israel of God" has assumed its final form until his "coming again," the consummation of all things.

# II

## JESUS AND THE CHURCH

THERE is a view with regard to Jesus and the church which I confess I have never been quite able to understand. This position may be stated, in the words of Bishop Barnes, thus: "In the opinion of the large majority of independent scholars, Jesus neither instituted sacraments nor founded a Church."[1] Neither is his meaning made clearer when he goes on to define "an independent scholar" as "one who does not feel bound to reach conclusions prescribed by the Christian communion to which he belongs." I should have thought that since the dawn of historical objectivity in the latter half of the nineteenth century, and more especially since the turn of the century, all scholars who were worthy of being called scholars were more or less in this category. At any rate, he cannot mean present-day scholars, for there is hardly a present-day New Testament scholar of eminence who, so far as the church is concerned, would agree with the statement that Jesus never founded a church. Indeed, the trend of scholarship since Harnack's day has been in the other direction. But perhaps he means by "independent scholars" those who, like himself, are able to produce the most startling and disturbing theories, based upon the flimsiest grounds—so far as grounds of scholarship are concerned—and often upon no grounds at all except the desire to have it so. Of this he gives us himself a fantastic example in his dissection of the first Corinthian letter into "a short genuine letter into which a bundle of notes, fly sheets and memoranda has been inserted."[2] In the field of scholarship, there is no more virtue in reaching conclusions which are rejected by the Christian communion to which one belongs than in reaching conclusions prescribed by the Christian communion to which one belongs. The only thing which makes a man a sound scholar in the examination of ancient documents is to be able to see *what is actually there*, whether he likes it or not, and apart altogether from whether it echoes the beliefs of his own communion or, on the other hand, provides a mild sensation in the ranks of the orthodox. Certainly the temptation to do the latter has vitiated the findings of scholars more frequently than the temptation to follow the path of orthodoxy, at least so far as the nineteenth century is concerned.

Let us return to the claim that Jesus never founded the church, a claim which was popular enough forty years ago, when the work of Harnack still had the glow of freshness about it[3] but which today is no longer seriously advanced in the name of New Testament scholarship. If it is made in the interests of that kind of Christianity, which is familiar enough in our day, and which claims that the gospel is one thing and the church quite another—that one can have the gospel without the church and can have Christianity as an individualistic religion without reference to the Christian community—then it ought to be obvious to any reader of the Bible that such a position is purely and simply a reflection into the past of a present position, a creation of "a past which never was a present." From the biblical point of view, to think in such an individualistic way is inconceivable. It is extremely doubtful whether such a way of thinking was possible before the seventeenth century; and, whether we regard it as a right way of thinking or not, we have no right to transpose it over the New Testament and then claim that the New Testament echoes our preferences. Such noncommunal thinking is foreign to the whole Bible, as it was foreign to the first generation of Protestant Reformers in the sixteenth century.[4] From this point of view, Jesus does not have *to found* a church: he comes with the church or in the church—the Israel of God—and as the Son of David he is part of the church.

If, on the other hand, it means no more than that Jesus, during his earthly life, did not found an ecclesiastical organization—complete with creed, sacraments, and machinery for discipline—the statement is innocent enough and need cause no alarm. Not even the most rabid ecclesiastic today, if at the same time he be a scholar, makes the claim that the church in its fully developed form came from the hands of Jesus himself. I suspect, however, that it means much more than this. I suspect that most of those who make the claim, do so in the interests of the view that Jesus, during his earthly life, was himself unconscious of any other function to be fulfilled by him than that of a prophet (though undoubtedly the greatest of the prophets) to his own people, calling them back to repentance and righteousness. Presumably, on this view, his work was to *reform* the old Israel, not to *create* a new Israel and, by so doing, fulfill the prophets who had preceded him. It is not my purpose here to argue this problem in all its complicated detail. I would, in the first place, refer the reader to an exhaustive discussion of the whole subject in Professor William Manson's book, *Jesus the Messiah*, and further say that so far as present-day scholarship is concerned, the weight of it is decidedly against the type of "reduced Christ" which is here envisaged and against the view that, in this sense, Jesus never founded a church.[5]

[ 38 ]

In the second place, I would say that the argument that Jesus' task was the reform of the old Israel and not the creation of a new Israel may be sound enough in one sense, for if the old Israel had not rejected him and had become reformed (in the sense in which he desired to *re-form* it, which certainly involved some kind of *crisis,* rather than mere evolutionary reform), it would have become the new Israel.[6] On this point Dr. C. J. Cadoux has said:*

> Now it is certainly true that Jesus at first expected to be able to win the whole nation, and that right on almost to the end he clung to the hope that possibly he might succeed. At the same time, he was not blind to the numerous indications which experience from time to time gave him of the improbability—or virtual impossibility—of his hope being realized; and he must have been familiar, through his knowledge of the Old Testament, with the prophetic idea of the Righteous Remnant, the nucleus of loyal Israelites who were "Israelites indeed," and through whom alone God's purpose for his Chosen People would be realized. Indeed, there is good reason for believing that, in fusing together the two conceptions of "the Son of Man" and the suffering "Servant of the Lord," he was envisaging as "the Son of Man" a corporate or social unit, consisting of the saved and saving Remnant of Israel with himself as its leader. In any case there would be nothing impossible in his deliberately contemplating and forming such a social group, while at the same time keeping hold of the hope

---

*The Historic Mission of Jesus,* pp. 306f.  Used by permission of the Lutterworth Press and Mr. T. J. Cadoux.

that it might possibly come to consist of the nation as a whole. Certain it is that Jesus constantly thought of his followers in terms of a community; and in so doing and in planning for its corporate life during his absence, he may in a certain sense of the words be described as deliberately founding a church.

Unless our Synoptic criticism is so negative that we are to abandon all hope of ever discovering any kind of Jesus as a historical Figure, it seems clear that Jesus called upon men to forsake father and mother, wife, family, wealth, and position for the sake of his name; to defy governors and even give up their lives for his sake. That the word "church" is not upon his lips, except in the two Matthean passages previously referred to, which find no support in any other Gospel, seems to me to be of small importance. Nowhere in the Synoptic Gospels does Jesus explicitly say that God is love, but who would want to claim that this, too, along with the idea of the church itself, was an invention of the apostolic church? It is implied in everything he says and does. Similarly, nowhere in the Synoptic Gospels is the word *charis* (grace) used in its Pauline sense of the free self-giving mercy of God, with the possible exception of Luke 17:9, yet most of the parables of Jesus and the whole action of his life are full of the idea. In the same way, his Parable of the Tower Builder and Par-

able of the King Who Went to War without Count-
ing the Cost are clearly aimed at teaching the devotion
due to himself by those who were to be his disciples.
"No monarch with invincible armies at his beck and
call could have asked of his subjects more unstinted
sacrifices in his service."" It seems clear that loyalty
to himself and to his mission are equated by Jesus
with loyalty to God; and that loyalty certainly meant
the founding of a society which was separate from the
world (a called-out society, which is what *ecclēsia*
means) and which eventually, because of the rejection of him by Temple and Synagogue, was to be
separate from the old Israel, though its true fulfillment and successor as God's missionary instrument
in the world.

Now let us look a little deeper, remembering what
has been previously said in Chapter I that the necessity and nature of the church are grounded in the fact
of revelation. Let us look at that revelation of the
purpose and character of God which is given, not in
the *teaching* of Jesus, but in the *action* of Jesus. In
the Marcan Gospel his ministry is divided into three
periods, more or less clearly defined, and these periods
are followed in the main outline by both Luke and
Matthew. I suggest that each is characterized by a
different method of teaching. The first period is that

of the Galilean ministry, mainly devoted to *public open* teaching and acts of mercy. The Parable of the Sower is almost certainly a reflection of Jesus upon its success and failure. Toward the end of this period he chooses from his followers twelve men "to be with him." These words, "to be with him," are certainly significant. At the end of this first period we find him alone with these twelve beyond the confines of Jewry. He seeks solitude with them. He is teaching now, not openly to the crowds and by word of mouth, but by *fellowship*, by living together with the group. It was a period of quiet meditation and intimate *sharing of personality*. Even Plato knew that no deep truth could be conveyed by word of mouth alone, still less by a written symbol. Jesus knows it, too. Of this rich *sharing* we have only glimpses here and there, far too few, but glimpses sufficient to give some idea of its beauty and costingness. He was making a bid for fellowship with this heterogeneous group, made up of a "collaborator" and an extreme nationalist, together with one who approximated to an anarchist; of fishermen of the well-to-do owner class and of the workman class; of a scientific-minded unbeliever like Thomas and of a guileless innocent like Nathanael. Here was the church in embryo, and it was a typical church at that. This is what *fellowship* means, not

[ 42 ]

the gathering together of a group of like-minded un-
interesting people calculated to bore anyone other
than themselves, but the nonexplosive interlocking of
those rich differences of personality which, if left to
themselves or organized on a class basis, would lead
to endless strife. Here, already, is that community
which is to know neither Jew nor Greek, neither bond
nor free, neither male nor female. At the end of this
period we find the disciples with Jesus at Caesarea
Philippi and for the first time we hear the Messianic
Confession on their lips, though as yet they ill understand its true significance. Still, their insight has
deepened: they have come that far. Note that this
is a *secret* for the inner community. To these men
"it has been given to know the secrets of the kingdom" and not yet to those outside. There is no
understanding of this apart from the fact that Jesus
was intentionally setting up a community to be his
church.

The third period of his ministry opens with his
announcement of the Passion and its rejection by the
disciples. From now on he struggles to make them
understand what is involved in a *suffering* Messiah,
an idea which was alien to their Jewish thought. In
this last period, he is, in the main, teaching by *action*.
By the most divine acts of witness, he shows them that

in a true fellowship, love rules by service and not by power, for God was never so great as when he stooped so low. He shows them that in charitable-mindedness, love o'erleaps the hard and fast boundaries which law and logic set up. And yet, such was the sorrow-laden path which now he trod, that we find him nearing Jerusalem, with all the aching weight of human sin and folly bearing him down, and these same disciples so oblivious to it all that they are actually quarreling among themselves as to who shall have first place in the kingdom. Already they are at work casting lots for his seamless robe of fellowship and unity. Here in their hearts at such a time is the very spirit which he had come to banish from the world forever —a spirit which still holds us bound in its chains. And so, he who had a greater capacity than any for fellowship must go to the cross *alone*—must die in utter loneliness, for "all the disciples forsook him and fled"— must die that the spirit which makes for fellowship might live forever and be reborn in the hearts of men and women the world over. And so, after Calvary, the church began, or "re-began," as *the fellowship;* and the Greek word *koinōnia* became filled with a new content, because Jesus had lived and died and risen again. Thus the church, in its deepest meaning, is now the revelation on the plane of history of the divine fellowship, witnessing to the fact that the hidden structure of reality is *fellowship*. No wonder that in the Fourth Gospel the Lord is declared to have prayed that the church might be one! But this is to anticipate.

This vivid teaching of Jesus by *action*, which is conveyed by the Synoptic account of his life, cannot be ignored. We shall see that it is confirmed by his teaching by word, but here it may be remarked that the conclusion to which it leads with reference to the church is not different from the teaching about the church which we have in Paul and in the Fourth Gospel. They are only saying in a different way what was a felt reality in the church from the beginning and, indeed, what undoubtedly goes back to the mind and action of Jesus himself.

When we turn to the actual teaching of Jesus as given in the Synoptic Gospels, we must remember that today we are no longer moving in the atmosphere of *Oxford Studies in the Synoptic Problem* (1911), much less in the atmosphere of the liberal criticism of the last half of the nineteenth century. With regard to the German criticism of that period, there is a good deal of truth in Dr. Blunt's dictum that "their theories seemed to explain everything except the existence of the Christian religion and of the

Christian church."[8]   We may best see the difference
of temper by placing over against this estimate of the
criticism of a generation ago the judgment of such a
sound and searching scholar as Dr. C. J. Cadoux
(1941): "Now let it be willingly conceded that the
historical data concerning Jesus embrace more than
the Synoptic Gospels, that they embrace the creation
of the Christian Church from an impulse which he
imparted."[9]   One of the main differences between
Synoptic studies of today and those of thirty or forty
years ago is that today we realize far more deeply
the part played in the mind of Jesus and in the writing of the Gospels by Old Testament ideas.[10]   We
realize that, though the New Testament was written in Greek, the ideas are mainly Semitic.

In this connection we must look at an important
piece of evidence relating to a saying of Jesus about
the temple.  Evidence is brought at the trial of Jesus
that he had spoken against the temple (*naos*), a blas-
phemous act for any Jew.  "We heard him say, 'I will
destroy this temple that is made with hands, and in
three days I will build another, not made with hands' "
(Mark 14:58; cf. Matt. 26:61).  The witnesses were
confused as to what he had said, and in that sense the
witness was false, but not in the sense that he had not
said something about destroying the temple.  Later

in Mark we are told that as our Lord hung upon the cross, the passers-by railed on him, "wagging their heads, and saying, 'Aha! You who would destroy the temple and build it in three days, save yourself, and come down from the cross!'" (15:29-30). In the Synoptic Gospels no such saying about the temple is attributed to Jesus, but in the Fourth Gospel we have an actual saying attributed to him: "Destroy this temple, and in three days I will raise it up" (John 2:19). We cannot be certain, with no more evidence than we have, as to exactly what Jesus had said, but it is clear that in some sense he regarded his cause as equivalent to the temple. This meaning is further emphasized in Mark's Gospel by the rending of the veil of the temple at the moment of Christ's death. I hardly think that Canon W. J. Phythian-Adams is too fanciful when he suggests: "In that hour (so we are to understand) a new Covenant was inaugurated in the Blood of the Servant (XIV, 24), and therefore in that same hour the old Sanctuary of the Presence ceased to 'have standing' (Heb. IX, 8). The 'Lord' had indeed 'come suddenly to His Naos,' both to build and to destroy."[11] In a very real sense the church is now to take the place of the temple as the place of the Presence of God. We are reminded of Paul's later understanding of the church as a holy temple (1 Cor. 3:16f.; 2 Cor. 6:16; Eph. 2:19-22), an understanding which is undoubtedly founded upon a genuine tradition of a word of Jesus. The kind of language which Paul here uses is not so remote from the teaching of Jesus as has often been supposed.

In a similar way the idea of the Kingdom of God is frequently upon the lips of Jesus. It is the great theme of his teaching and the theme of most of his parables in the Synoptic Gospels. It is definitely a Jewish idea. While the actual expression "Kingdom of God," or its equivalent "Kingdom of the Heavens," is infrequent in Jewish literature, there is plenty of evidence to show that the expectation of the coming of the kingdom dominated Jewish thinking of our Lord's day. No doubt most Jews of that day, and not only apocalyptic-minded Jews, looked for the kingdom to be ushered in by catastrophic events which would revolutionize the political scene. John the Baptist comes announcing its nearness. The beginning and the end of Jesus' ministry in Luke's Gospel are full of the anticipation of this event. Simeon looks for "the consolation of Israel" (2:25). The crowd was "looking for the redemption of Jerusalem" (2:38). At the end of his ministry Jesus deliberately staged the Triumphal Entry, and the crowds hailed him: "Blessed be the kingdom of our father David that is coming! Hosanna in the highest!" (Mark 11:10).

When speaking of the Kingdom of God, Jesus was using a phrase familiar to his hearers. This does not necessarily mean that he meant by the term what was popularly understood. It seems clear from the Gospels that, by teaching and parable, he was putting a content into the phrase that was not altogether familiar to his hearers. Fundamental to his thought, and to theirs, is the idea that God is King and that God has subjects. The term itself in the Aramaic and in the Greek does not express a "realm," as our word "kingdom" does, but rather a state of royalty and a sphere of discipline. It is important to note in the Synoptic Gospels certain sayings and parables which relate the kingdom to Jesus himself. These are rare, but one or two of them are fairly well authenticated. The best attested are the request of the mother that the two sons of Zebedee should sit, one on his right hand and one on his left hand (Matt. 20:21; Mark 10:37); the Parable of the Nobleman (Luke 19:12-27); and the saying of the thief on the cross (Luke 23:42). This conception of Christ as the Head of the kingdom dominates early Christian thought (1 Cor. 15:24; Eph. 5: 5; Col. 1:13; Rev. 1:9; John 18:36) and is obviously based on the fact which the Synoptic teaching, including the parables, clearly lays claim to, that Jesus is not only the bringer of news of the kingdom; he is himself the bringer of the kingdom, and in some sense the kingdom itself. What is unique about his teaching is the place which he himself holds in his own God consciousness. Whatever the kingdom is in the teaching of Jesus, it is obviously closely linked with the gospel (the good news of salvation) which he brings and which he is; and this "good news" involves the creation of a "people of God," the subjects of the kingdom—if you will, a church.

While we may use the expression "the Kingdom of God" in a wider sense than the church, there is really no evidence that as used in the Synoptic Gospels it differed from what was later meant by the *ecclēsia* (the called-out people). It seems to me perfectly clear that when we pass over to the Pauline Epistles, kingdom and church are closely identified and that we do not have to wait till St. Augustine for the identification.[12]   That Jesus regarded his mission as related to the coming of the Kingdom of God is proof enough that he regarded it as related to a corporate society of those who owed allegiance to God and were to be under the discipline of his law, whether that law were Torah or *agapē*.

Finally, let us note three characteristic things about his teaching concerning the kingdom. First, for him the kingdom is already present in his day;[13] and yet it is still to come.[14] It is a state of being and becoming. This seeming contradiction is distinctly Semitic and alien to the Greek mind. It is only possible to entertain it if we are looking at the kingdom as a dynamic entity. It is ever on the march, but not necessarily to a goal on in front. In one sense, the goal is as much behind as in front. It is rooted in those sublime events which had happened in history, the *eschaton* which gave Christians confidence in every struggle. Armageddon, which has been such a sorry stumbling block, for early Christians was not on in front; it was already behind. Being a dynamic thing, the kingdom never reaches a state of stable equilibrium. Being like its Lord, it is, in this world, a *living* pulsating thing, fashioned by history, yet fashioning it, eternity "struck down" into time and ever moving toward its eternal goal.

Secondly, the kingdom is not of this world,[15] and yet it certainly has to do with this world. What this appears to mean is that the kingdom (church) does not take *political* shape as a state does.[16] It is a new order of men and women without distinction of race and class,[17] inspired by a new motive, the motive of love and service. It is quite definitely a *visible* corporation, though at any given moment it includes both the church on earth and the church in heaven. It has a definite destiny in history, subordinate ends to accomplish, but its consummation is beyond history.

Thirdly, the way of its working is not that of gradualness but of *leaven*. It is the "salt of the earth," the leaven which "leavens the whole lump." As "salt," the church is set in the world to preserve the world from utter corruption.[18] As "leaven," the church is really explosive material in the world, though it may appear to be working quietly, and is often working in a hidden way. Constantly the world comes to "ripe times," "fulfilled times," "comings of the Son of man," in which the choice between two alternatives, both relative "goods" and therefore evils, is transcended and a new ethical level is reached. The church is "the carrier of possibilities," which, in her own life, become actualized and, through her life, transform the world. The true church is the church related to the *future*, and she can dare to be so related to the future because she is so deeply rooted in the past.[19]

This conception of the church, which seems to me to be clear in the teaching of Jesus, means that the church is not so much the "ark of salvation" as the "bringer of salvation"; not only the kingdom of God's mercy and redemption, but the instrument of his mercy and redemption. The "good news of salvation," the "sure mercies of David," which Jesus brings, turns out to be the coming of Jesus himself, his incarnation, death, burial, resurrection, exaltation, his sending of the Holy Spirit and establishing of his church. In these acts, including the act of bringing the church, it was said that God had "visited and redeemed his people."

# III

## THE CHURCH IN THE TEACHING
## OF PAUL

It IS one of the paradoxes of the Christian religion that Paul, who can be described as "the classic exponent of the idea of freedom and universality in religion,"[1] is yet the one in the New Testament to whom we owe the most profound doctrine of the church, we might say, of "the one holy catholic apostolic church"—of the church as the corporate society of the saved and saving remnant of Israel. The day is past when Paul could be interpreted, as was common in many interpretations a generation ago, as the champion of that kind of Protestant individualism which knows Christianity without the church. That this was a common type of Protestant Christianity in the nineteenth century and the early years of the present century, cannot be denied. It was, let it be said, a debased Protestantism, judged even by the standards of the eighteenth century, to say nothing of the great Protestant Confessions of the sixteenth and seventeenth centuries.

Over against this overindividualistic interpretation of Paul, the radical criticism of the latter half of the nineteenth century had seen quite clearly that Paul was a kind of institutionalist and a sacramentalist. Great ingenuity was spent in trying to prove that the roots of his institutionalism and sacramentalism were to be found in the Hellenic culture in which he moved and more especially in the mystery cults.[2] Apart from the doubtful conjecture as to its sources, this was a more realistic picture of Paul,[3] but it was a picture quite unpalatable to the Protestant mind of the day. Hence the cry, "Back to Jesus," which meant "back to Jesus away from Paul." From then on, the fashion in critical circles was to set Jesus and Paul in almost complete opposition.[4] It was a thankless task, this setting of Jesus and his greatest follower in complete opposition. From the beginning, it was beset with difficulties as was seen by Johannes Weiss' defense of Paul.[5] Gradually it became clear, even to liberal scholars, that the kind of opposition envisaged by such scholars as Arnold Meyer and Weinel was a distortion of the actual, historical situation.[6] Whatever Paul was, he could not be taken as the first perverter of the original gospel.

Despite all this, it was still possible for a scholar like A. T. Robertson, in his book, *Paul the Interpreter of Christ* (1921), to put forward the older rather individualist nonchurchly interpretation of Paul, reflecting back on him the Protestant prejudices of his day.[7] With the passing of another twenty-five years and the deeper knowledge we now have, both of the Hellenistic environment in which Paul moved and of the Jewish background from which he came, all this seems to us today rather antiquated and out of touch with historical reality. The fact is, of course, that Paul, like every Jewish prophet, was an individualist in a very real sense, but an individualist *in community*. Of that kind of individualism with which we are familiar, which is able to conceive of a man's being a Christian out of relationship to the people of God, he knew nothing and could know nothing. Nor would that kind of Christianity which is able to conceive of the gospel as separate from the church have been intelligible to him. That he could ever have been taken as the champion of individualistic nonchurchly Protestantism is one of the ironies of history. That he was the champion of the deeper spiritual interpretation of the gospel which inspired St. Augustine and the Protestant Reformers is quite a different thing, and true enough. But the Christianity of St. Augustine, and that of Luther and Calvin, was a churchly Christianity, as was that of Paul. For Paul, there could no more be the gospel without the church than there could be the Messiah without the Messianic community. True, the gospel had created the church, but the church was part of the gospel, as the Messianic community was inseparable from the Messiah.

Paul did not create the church nor the church idea. It was already there for him to be admitted into after he had done his best by persecution to destroy it. If we may rely on the account given in the early chapters of Acts,[3] it was gathered together from the scattered disciples at the time of the Crucifixion by the Resurrection appearances of our Lord. Apart from the Resurrection, it is impossible to explain the appearance of the church. Indeed, it consists of those Jews, loyal Jews in all other respects, it would seem, who, through his Resurrection, regard Jesus of Nazareth as God's long-promised Messiah and the Redeemer of his people Israel. Between the Ascension and Pentecost they are gathered together in Jerusalem, and after Pentecost they preach to the people this same truth. In all other respects they are Jews like their brethren, and yet they were conscious of a new creation, a new corporate loyalty, of being, as it were, "Israel within Israel,"which was in a new relationship to God, a new relationship made possible through Jesus of Nazareth. And all this which had happened was a direct fulfillment of prophecy (Acts 2:16-39; 3:13-26).

This new society had its own rite of initiation—baptism in the name of Jesus Christ—and its own fellowship worship—"the breaking of bread and the prayers"—as well as its own daily school of instruction after the manner of the synagogue (Acts 2:42). Like other ancient corporations, it also had its own system of corporate discipline (Acts, chap. 5), and its means of social economy (Acts 2:43-47). If it was a sect within Jewry, and no doubt it was at first so regarded by those without, it was more than a sect. Indeed, it was "the leaven," the ferment which was set in Jewry to transform it. But it was a "leaven" which was *visible*, which could be added to (Acts 2:41, 47) and not a mere reform idea. Men and women were added to it by its own peculiar rite of initiation and could be identified by a form of worship and its own "way of life." Indeed, it would appear that it came to be known as "the Way" (Acts 9:2). It was a society of Jews who believed that Jesus of Nazareth was not only the Messiah, but Lord (*Kyrios*) as well (Acts 2:36), the "Servant of the Lord" of Second Isaiah, "the Holy and Righteous One," "the Author of Life" (Acts 3:14-15), whom the heavens had received "until the time for establishing all that God" had promised (Acts 3:21). Further, he was "the stone which the builders had rejected," which was made "the head of the corner" (Acts 4:11; Psalm 118:22), and in none other name was there salvation.

The church could already be described as "their own company" (Acts 4:23, A.V.), a body to whom a report could be given; servants of the Lord, possessed of a word to be preached with all boldness in the face of persecution; it could be described as "of one heart and soul" and possessing all things in common, with a definite body of officials—the apostles—who were in charge of both doctrine and finance (Acts 4:32-37).

In Acts 5:11 we meet, for the first time, the word *ecclēsia* applied to this corporate society, and from then on it is in frequent use. It had been the normal word used in the Septuagint to translate the Hebrew words *edah* and *qāhāl*, which meant Israel as a corporate society. Undoubtedly the word as applied to the followers of Christ already means that here is the "new Israel" of God, whom he has "called out" to be his own peculiar people. From now on it becomes the normal word denoting this community. Throughout Acts, with one exception (20:28), the expression "the church" is used without any other qualification such as "church of Christ" or "church of God." This would seem to imply that the bare expression, "the church," was already familiar as setting the Christian community over against the synagogue. Already the distinction between church and synagogue, which was later to play such an important part, was becoming manifest, and that on Palestinian soil.

Note also that the word *ecclēsia* is first used in the singular before it is used in the plural. The *one* church is before the churches. Not until Acts 15:41 do we find the expression "the churches." This is not due, as might be supposed, to the fact that we have to wait for the Pauline missionary movement before there were more churches than one. In this connection, Acts 9:31 is significant. In the best Greek texts, followed by all modern versions, *ecclēsia* is in the singular. In the American Revised Standard Version the text reads: "So the church throughout all Judea and Galilee and Samaria had peace and was built up." Here it is *one* church, though obviously meeting in different congregations. Likewise, when particular local churches are referred to, they are referred to as "*the* church in Jerusalem" (Acts 11:22) or "*the* church at Antioch" (Acts 13:1). The one church is not the collection of separate churches, but the separate churches are the expression of the one church in different localities. This usage is so striking in Acts that it cannot be ignored. Let it be said at once that it tells heavily against a certain type of congregationalism or independency. Dr. A. E. Garvie outlined three kinds of congregationalism, which he called "Broad," "Low," and "High."[9] The first thought of the church as merely an association of like-minded people, such as a Rotary Club, a conception which is barbarous with the New Testament in our hands. The second made the association to be under the guidance of the Spirit, with the local society so formed under no other authority. The third, which was Dr. Garvie's own type, thought of the local congregation as *a* church because it was the local manifestation of *the one* church.[10] This is the only theological formulation of congregationalism which is compatible with what we have here in Acts, and it is the theological formulation which is today held by such Congregationalist scholars as Dr. Nathaniel Micklem, Dr. John S. Whale, Dr. C. H. Dodd, and was held by the late Bernard Lord Manning.

The church in this pre-Pauline stage is at first composed of Palestinian Jews and Hellenistic Jews (Greek-speaking Jews). But already, resulting from persecution and the martyrdom of Stephen, missionary work has been begun among Samaritans and proselytes, if not among actual Gentiles, before Saul, the archpersecutor of the church, is converted and admitted as a member. Already the distinction is clear between two worlds—the world of "the wrath to come," and the world of the redeemed; the world of evil-doers, and the world of "the saints" or "holy ones"; the world of the prince of darkness, and the world of the Prince of peace and King of kings. A visible society,[11] organized as one body, but appearing in different localities; possessed of certain world-shattering beliefs; practicing a rite of initiation and a rite of worship; manifesting a peculiar way of life, both within the society and publicly in the world; under the pastoral care and teaching of a definite body of men, is set in the world as the "new creation" of God in Christ, guided and empowered by the Holy Spirit to withstand all resistance. All this is to receive definite theological formulation in the writings of Paul, but already we have that divine creation, "the one holy catholic apostolic church," which is to spread throughout the world and against which "the gates of Hades" (death and worse than death) have no power.

All these ideas and their actuality, Paul must have found in existence when, by his baptism, he was admitted to the church in Damascus. In the stress of a busy missionary life, with its adversities and perils; in a major conflict with the Judaizers in the church, whose center was Jerusalem; in opposition to the prevailing syncretism of the Hellenic world in which he preached the gospel of redemption; and on the background of strife and failure within the Christian society, he it was who gave to these ideas a more precise theological formulation. What he quite definitely does not do is to create the ideas. They were already there. But what he does do, with his spiritual genius and intellectual equipment, is to see more fully the implications of them and to give them permanent form.

[ 63 ]

This we find done for us in the *occasional* letters of a busy missionary and not in a systematic treatise in theological form.[12] It is important to recognize this. It means that the deepest truths about the church are often almost casually conveyed by Paul without argument and belong to those things which are accepted without question between the writer and the reader of a letter. It is also important to note that each one of these letters, with the exception of that to Philemon, is written to a church, and not to an individual or group of individuals. Even Philemon is not without mention of "the church in your house" (vs. 2); and Philippians, which mentions bishops and deacons, mentions the church first (1:1). The expressions used for "the church" in the opening of the letters vary: "church of the Thessalonians" (1 Thess. 1:1; 2 Thess. 1:1), "the churches of Galatia" (Gal. 1:2), "the church of God which is at Corinth" (1 Cor. 1:2; 2 Cor. 1:1), "all God's beloved in Rome, who are called to be saints" (Rom. 1:7), "all the saints in Christ Jesus who are at Philippi" (Phil. 1:1), "the saints and faithful brethren in Christ at Colossae" (Col. 1:2), "the saints who are also faithful in Christ Jesus" (Eph. 1:1); but each letter is written to the corporate society as such. Especially is it important to remember that "the saints"[13] is a collective expression in the same way that "the children of Israel" and "sons of God" are collective expressions. The fact that, later, the church came to apply the word "saint" to special individuals has led us to read back into the Pauline letters an individualistic interpretation of many passages which to him could have had no such meaning.[14] A striking example of this is given in a well-known hymn based on the glowing passage in Ephesians 3:17-18: "That Christ may dwell in your hearts through faith; that you, being rooted and grounded in love, may have power to comprehend *with all the saints* what is the breadth and length and height and depth, and to know the love of Christ which surpasses knowledge, that you may be filled with all the fullness of God." Mary Shekleton's hymn completely ignores "with all the saints," without which the passage is lacking in meaning, and assumes that this knowledge, this inscrutable mystery, is possible for a single Christian apart from the fellowship of the saints in all ages and all places:

> It passeth knowledge, that dear love of thine,
> My Saviour Jesus! yet this soul of mine
> Would of Thy love, in all its breadth and length,
> Its height and depth, its everlasting strength,
> Know more and more.

It is this kind of thing which has done despite to much that Paul wrote, but let none suppose that it is a peculiar Protestant heresy. Mary Shekleton can be matched by much in the medieval mystics. Indeed, the notion of the corporeity of the church, at least in the West, is waning from the fifth century onward, especially in the sense of the church as *fellowship*. There is a very real sense in which it can be said that both Luther and Calvin in part recovered it.

The paradox of the one and the many is ever with the church. Paul was ever aware of it. He refers to it in connection with the Lord's Supper: "Because there is one loaf, we who are many are one body, for we all partake of the same loaf" (1 Cor. 10:17). It is as individuals that we accept Christ and become members of the church, but immediately we are more than individuals; we are members of his body and, because of that, members of one another. We are not solitary individuals. There is a togetherness which we ignore at our peril.

It has sometimes been claimed that a "high" doctrine of the church is found only in the later Epistles of Paul—Philippians, Colossians, and Ephesians—and does not appear in the earlier group. Such a claim cannot be maintained. It is true that little is found in the Thessalonian letters and perhaps not much more in Galatians, but the Corinthian correspondence and Romans leave nothing to be desired. We must remember that by the year 54, if not before, Paul was having to deal with a threatened serious split within the church and that later, in his prison letters, he was having to deal with a serious threat from without, what he calls an "empty deceit."[15]   But while this, no doubt, caused him to dwell more explicitly on the doctrine of the church, its unity and indissoluble corporeity, it would be hazardous to conclude that this same doctrine was not implicitly held by both Paul and his readers in the Thessalonian letters, especially knowing the tradition concerning the church which Paul himself received when he entered it.   Even in the Thessalonian letters it is quite definitely stated that Christians are "the elect of God" (1 Thess. 1:4; 2 Thess. 2:13, A.V.); they are exhorted to "hold to the traditions" which were current in the church (2 Thess. 2:15); and both letters give us a picture of an organized community with its forms of discipline (2 Thess. 3:6).   The case is even more clear in Galatians, where the threat to unity is already severe, and where one can see Paul—the individualist, if you like—anxious to maintain the liberty which is in Christ Jesus against an older restricting tradition, and yet careful to do nothing to create a breach between the mother church and the younger churches of the Gentile mission.   Here Paul develops that interpretation of history in which Christians become "sons of Abraham" (Gal. 3:7) and heirs of "the blessings of Abraham" in Christ Jesus (Gal. 3:14), and culminates in the conception of the church as "the Israel of God" (Gal. 6:16), the "true Israel" of promise over against the "false Israel" of flesh, the one Israel which includes both Jew and Gentile. But, if this is said of Christians, it is said of Christians as "all one in Christ Jesus" (Gal. 3:28), as the community of the "sons of God," who are no longer servants but are now able to cry "Abba!" (Gal. 4:6).[16] This is as clear as it is later in Ephesians.

In Corinthians we meet with three fruitful mystical realities—I say "realities" for they are more than metaphors. The church is described as God's "fellow workmen," "God's field," and "God's building" (1 Cor. 3:9). All three are Semitic in origin. The first is derived from the notion that Israel of old was chosen by God to fulfill his missionary purpose in the world.[17] The second derives from the familiar prophetic understanding of Israel as God's vineyard.[18] It has a parallel in Paul's reference to the olive tree in Romans 11:17-24. The idea of Christ as the Vine of God and the church, in Christ, being the branches of the Vine becomes dominant in Christian thinking from now on.[19] The third receives further expansion in the third chapter of 1 Corinthians and appears elsewhere in Paul's writings. The church is a building founded on Christ (1 Cor. 3:11), and yet founded on apostles and prophets (Eph. 2:20). It is the temple of God for God's habitation through the Spirit (1 Cor. 3:16-17; Eph. 2:22). Not only is the church the temple of God, but each Christian, as a member of the church, becomes a temple of the Holy Spirit, which doctrine Paul makes the basis of his Christian ethic, for the temple must not be defiled (1 Cor. 6:19). Behind all this lies the definitely Hebrew idea, in its Christian form, that in the Incarnation and the establishing of the church, God has come to his holy temple.

From this idea of the church as God's building, an idea which carries its own dangers of being too *static* a conception, dangers which Paul himself probably recognized, it is an easy transition to his most fruitful and more organic conception of the church as the body of Christ, the instrument by which he now performs his will. The expression appears for the first time in 1 Corinthians and becomes from then on his most common way of referring to the church. It has often been spoken of as a metaphor, but his usage demands that we regard it as more than a metaphor. It demands a concept of "identity with difference." It is of a mystical reality that Paul speaks. For him, there are three bodies connected with Christ: the body of his flesh (Rom. 7:4; Col. 1:22), that is, of the Incarnation; the body which is given in the bread of the Eucharist (1 Cor. 10:16-17; 11:24, 29); and the body which is the church (1 Cor. 6:12-20; 12:12-13; Rom. 12:

4.5; Col. 1:18-20, 24; Eph. 1:22-23). In all three there is "identity with difference." It also involves the notion that because we are members of Christ's body, the church, we are members of one another (Rom. 12:5). So far is this identification carried that in 1 Corinthians 12:12, Paul uses the expression "the Christ" to mean "the church." Here "the Christ" means, not the exalted Jesus alone, but the exalted Jesus plus those who are "with him," his saints. The same identity is implied in Colossians and Ephesians, though not expressly stated as it is in the Corinthian passage. Christ is the Head of the body, but he is also the whole body, including the church, which constitutes the "members" of his body other than the Head. As we shall see later, the same understanding lies behind the Johannine conception of Christ as the True Vine (John 15:1-11).

Whence Paul derived this understanding of the church as the body of Christ, which is his most fruitful idea, is a matter of conjecture. It may be that there lies behind it Ezekiel's vision of the dry bones.[20] It is possible, however, that he was influenced by the words of institution at the Last Supper, "this is my body," and that this is revealed in his meditations in 1 Corinthians, chapters 10 and 11. Certainly in all that he writes, his mind is influenced by the close relationship between the sacraments of baptism and the Lord's Sup-

per, on the one hand, and the church or the body of
Christ, on the other hand, and the relationship of each
Christian, who is a member of the church, to the Incarnate Christ and to the Spirit whom he sends. What
happens to Christ in the flesh, happens to the Christian.
Christ in the flesh dies, he is buried, he rises from the
dead by the power of God. In baptism, Christians die,
they are buried, they are raised again by the same
power of God. Christ suffers: Christians suffer with
him. It is coexperiencing. Similarly, in the Eucharist there is this same coexperiencing of the things per-
taining to Christ's suffering. What happens in the
rite becomes significant for the whole life of those who
are in the body of Christ. In Colossians he goes so
far as to say, "Now I rejoice in my sufferings for your
sake, and in my flesh I complete what remains of
Christ's afflictions *for the sake of his body, that is, the
church*" (1:24). This passage has caused the com-
mentators great trouble, if not anguish, for at first
sight it looks like a kind of blasphemy. But it is no
idle boast on Paul's part. He is setting forth the common life of the church. Christ still lives on in the
church, which is his body, and though his redemptive
work was triumphantly accomplished in the days of
his flesh, Christians suffer here with him and in him
until "the time of restitution of all things" (Acts 3:
21, A.V.), and this suffering is shared both in the

worship of the church—baptism and the Lord's Supper—and in its life. It is "for the sake of his body, that is, the church" that Paul can be said "to complete what remains of Christ's afflictions."

From the idea of the church as the body of Christ, it is but an easy step to the idea of the church as the bride of Christ. This finds its classic expression in Ephesians 5:22-33, where it is spoken of as a great mystery,[21] and becomes the basis of a new understanding of Christian marriage. Here, quite definitely, Paul bases himself on the nuptial theology of Hosea, Jeremiah, and Second Isaiah (Hos. 2:14-20; Jer. 2:2; 3:8; Isa. 62:4-5). It enables Paul to put the relationship between Christ and the church in its most intimate form. It is no new creation of his, for it simply carries over to the "new Israel" what has been affirmed of the "old Israel," but, because of the Incarnation, it becomes even more intimate and much richer. It is a daring conception, only possible without grave disaster in religions which are soundly ethical, as is the case with Judaism and Christianity. If not in Paul, certainly later, this, too, becomes closely related to the sacraments. So far as baptism is concerned, we may find a hint of this in Paul's statement, "for I betrothed you to Christ to present you as a pure bride to her one husband" (2 Cor. 11:2), where, for the church, baptism would stand in the place of the betrothals. So far as the Eucharist is concerned, we early meet with the idea that it is an antepast of the Lamb's Bridal Feast.[22]

In all this Paul thinks of the church as one (Eph. 4:4-6; 2:16; 1 Cor. 12:12-29) in the same way that the Father, Son, and Holy Spirit are one. Christ is not only the Head of the church but is identified with the church (Eph. 1:22; Col. 1:18). As men and women are in Christ by virtue of their being in the church, so the local church is a church because it is in the one church and is the outcrop of the one church in that particular place. So closely is the church identified with Christ that it shares his work as Judge. In what may seem to us fanciful language, Paul speaks of the church's destiny as including the judging of angels (1 Cor. 6:3) and making known "to the principalities and powers in the heavenly places" the mystery of God (Eph. 3:10). The church is constituted a body of "fellow heirs with Christ" (Rom. 8:17), who possess already the "first fruits" (*arrhabōn*) of the Spirit, or, as the writer of Hebrews puts it, have already "tasted . . . the powers of the age to come" (6:5), who are "God's elect" (Rom. 8:33, A.V.), commissioned of God, sealed by the Holy Spirit (2 Cor. 1:21-22), and the church is "the kingdom of God" (Rom. 14:16) and "the kingdom of his beloved Son" (Col. 1:13). All these exalted expressions find

[ 73 ]

their climax in the description given in Philippians 3:20, where the church is described as a "colony of heaven."[23] This expression must be understood in the Roman sense of a colony, as a piece of heaven planted down here on earth until the consummation of all things.

This constitutes the Pauline picture of the church —a living organism, gathered out of the world by God through Christ for his special purpose, a saved and saving remnant; made alive by *faith* in the living Christ; enduring all buffeting by the living *hope* that if they suffered with him, they would also be glorified with him (Rom. 8:17); and bound together by *agapē*, the divine charity which was the gift of God in Christ. If the members of the church, by virtue of their being members, were joined to Christ, they were also joined to one another (Rom. 12:5; Eph. 4:25), so that if one suffered, all suffered. There could be no escaping this corporeity, this togetherness, however the members might differ in individual gifts and graces. It was *koinōnia*, the essential nature of the church, because it was the hidden structure of reality, which the church was to manifest in the world.

# IV

## THE CHURCH IN THE JOHANNINE WRITINGS

IN THIS chapter I confine myself to the Fourth Gospel and the First Epistle of John. No attention is given to the Apocalypse, which is obviously by another hand. The Second and Third Epistles are too slight to be of any real value. The Gospel and the First Epistle stand together, whether they are by the same hand or by different hands, as Professor C. H. Dodd has suggested that they are, stating that the ideas are so similar that "we seem bound to conclude, either that the two writings are from one hand, or that the writer of the one was strongly influenced by the writer of the other, whether that influence was due to personal discipleship, or to a deep and prolonged study of his work, or to both."[1]

At first sight, when one looks at these writings, which belong to a generation after the time of Paul, one is inclined to think that the doctrine of the church is absent from them for they contain neither the word *ecclēsia* nor the term "body of Christ," the characteristic primitive and Pauline expressions for the church.[2] But it would be quite wrong to conclude that the writer (or writers) of these two documents was not interested in the *visible* church, as we shall show. E. F. Scott has shown how clearly the opposite is true, so far as the Gospel is concerned; and what is true for the Gospel is true also for the First Epistle.[3] It is true that, if one reads these writings without the consciousness of what has gone before, it is possible to read them as books of personal devotion addressed to in-dividual Christians, and that explains why they have been so used throughout the ages by Christians who sit loose to the idea of the church, and why it has been even possible to contend that they emanated from a Gnostic circle, which was not interested in the Incarna-tion, as such, nor in any kind of Christianity which was related to historical forms.[4]

In view of this, it might be well that I should state briefly my own position with regard to the Fourth Gospel. I hold that it comes from the province of proconsular Asia, probably in the last decade of the first century, but that it bears traces of Antiochian influence. I do not think that Dr. Torrey's claim that it was originally written in Aramaic and that what we have is a translation can be substantiated. But it undoubtedly contains more Aramaisms than any other document in the New Testament. Far from its being the most Hellenic document in the New Testament, it is in many ways more characteristically Jewish than the Gospel of Luke. Though the writer wrote in Greek, he thought in Aramaic. I hold, therefore, that the writer was a Jew, who was intimately acquainted with the topography of Palestine. Far from being uninterested in the Jesus of history, he uses the word "Jesus" more frequently than any of the Synoptic writers, even when the differing lengths of the Gospels are taken into account. He is even concerned at one or two places to correct false impressions which might be gathered from the Synoptics, as, for example, the day of the Last Supper and of the Crucifixion, and the length of the ministry. At other places he supplies historical data which are lacking in the Synoptics. It is most probable that he was at least acquainted with Mark's Gospel, if not with the other two. The Gospel is therefore based upon the reminiscences of a disciple of Jesus, whether he were an actual apostle or not.

I hold that the writer views the earthly ministry of Jesus from a different perspective from that of the Synoptics, but the difference is not that they give us a picture of the "historical Jesus" and that he gives us a picture of the "heavenly Christ." To all the Gospel writers, Jesus is the divine-human Figure, who is the Savior and Redeemer of men, though they may each use different language to describe this stupendous fact. The different perspective of this writer is a time perspective. He looks back upon the human figure of

Jesus from a different point of view, which has been created by a richer experience of the living Christ in the church and by the clearer way in which the divine-human nature of Jesus has been expressed, mainly owing to the Pauline theology. It does not follow that, because he is further removed from the historic Jesus than Mark, he will give a less accurate account of fact plus interpretation, which is in Mark as well as in John. It is possible to see things too "near up" as well as too "far off." In fact, it is possible to claim that in many cases he gives us an even more accurate account of events in the life of Jesus, especially if we mean by "accurate" the true significance of the events. There is a sense in which the difference between the Gospel of John and a Gospel like that of Mark may be illustrated by the difference between a cartographer's description of a tract of country and an artist's, though this must not be pressed too far; but would we say that the cartographer's account was true and the artist's untrue? Surely, they are both true in their own way. (I have in mind, of course, artists other than cubist or surrealist!)

I admit that in using dialogue and monologue to convey the teaching of Jesus, the writer is using a different literary artifice from that of the Synoptic writers, and that in doing so the teaching has much more relationship to the problems facing the church of his own day than has that of the Synoptics; but this does not admit of our drawing hasty negative conclusions as to whether the teaching goes back to the historic Jesus. The writer is surely right in pointing to a ministry of Jesus other than the Galilean ministry, which would involve a different kind of audience. Further, I admit that ideas in the teaching of Jesus which appear in the Synoptics are here clothed in different language, but it does not follow that the ideas themselves are different. The account of the teaching given often also involves a foreshortening of time, because this writer sees Jesus *sub specie aeternitatis*; but the content of the teaching, in its fundamental ideas, is not different, nor is the significance of the main facts in the life of Jesus—his Passion, his Resurrection and Exaltation, his sending of the Holy Spirit.

There is here also a deepening of the sense of mystery, awe, and wonder about the life of Jesus and the kingdom; but the mystery is not absent from a primitive Gospel like Mark (e.g., 4:10-12). The miracles are parables as well as miracles; but this is even a feature, less developed it is true, of the more primitive Gospels. Here symbolism, which is not absent from the Synoptics, especially Matthew and Mark, plays a greater part as a literary artifice. Indeed, there is a sense in which the whole Gospel is symbolic, or dramatic, as Strachan has claimed;[5] but this does not mean that it is not history. Furthermore, it is dynamic Hebraic symbolism and not essentially Hellenic. To illustrate, the writer is writing of the *eternal* Christ, who in one sense neither comes nor goes. Therefore Jesus neither comes nor goes: there is neither birth nor ascension in the Gospel, so far as actual historical narrative is concerned. But this does not mean that the writer did not accept the birth of Jesus or believe in his ascension and exaltation. Indeed, he it is who says, "the Word became flesh" (John 1:14), using the strongest and most anti-Docetic word to express his thought; and he it is who says: " 'I am going to him who sent me.' " " 'A little while, and you will not see me, and again a little while, and you will see me.' " " 'I go to the Father.' " (John 16: 5, 17.)

Finally, I hold that the Gospel is written with apologetic purpose and that this purpose is illuminated if we think of three groups opposing the church of his day: (*a*) the Jews who had rejected Jesus as the Messiah of God; (*b*) followers of John the Baptist, who regarded John as the True Light; (*c*) Docetic Christians, who had separated from the church but still acted within it like a "fifth column." These Christians viewed lightly the historicity of Jesus and, with true Hellenic mind, rejected the essential Hebraism and historicity of the Gospel, preferring the *spiritual* Christ. This itself makes it necessary for us to realize how intensely this writer was concerned for the unity of the one church in its visible manifestation and explains much which, on a cursory reading, is "hidden" in the Gospel concerning the church and its nature.

It will not be denied that this Gospel is the Gospel of the Incarnation, in which the Word of God assumes actual historical shape in the Person of Jesus of Nazareth. Whatever we are to say about the term "Logos," it is·certain that the idea of "the Word" in the mind of the writer is not adequately met by the Stoic conception of the universal Reason.[6] He has in mind the Semitic notion of the dynamic concrete Word of God, represented by the Hebrew *Davar* and the Aramaic *Memra*. I have previously claimed that the prologue can be interpreted as a kind of philosophy of history (see pp. 19ff.), which is conditioned by the idea of a "people of God," in whom the Word seeks to be incarnated. Here the church, the "Messianic community," the "Israel of God," is introduced as fulfilling, or failing to fulfill, its function in history, in three movements, in ever deepening intensity and increasing concretion, until it stands revealed in one Man, who is not only the beloved Son, the pre-existent Word, but is himself the "Messianic community," the "Israel of God," reduced to one Man. So the Gospel is introduced. It goes on to show that from this "center of history," there moves out into history again the same circles, but with this difference: the redemptive action of God has been completed, and God has been fully manifested. There is still the world, and there is still the church in the world, though not of the world, and there is still the "church within the church," that leaven which leavens, not only the church, but the world itself.

And so, after the prologue, the first chapter goes on to proclaim Jesus as the Lamb of God (John 1:29) and as the One who baptizes with the Holy Spirit (1:33). It is so easy to miss what is implied in these two assertions unless we are familiar with the development of ideas associated with the Jewish apocalyptic writings which emerged between 200 B.C. and A.D. 100.[7] Both these expressions are closely associated with Messianic ideas and with the Messianic community. The former points to the Messianic Banquet, which is a familiar theme in the Apocalypse of John and is referred to in connection with the Last Supper in Luke (22:15-17). This is the Lamb's Bridal Feast, which is shared with his bride, the church, already foreshadowed in the Parable of the Bridegroom (Matt. 25:1-13) and in the saying about fasting (Mark 2:19; Luke 5:34). I have already pointed out that the miracles in this Gospel are also parables, and I suggest that the story of the marriage feast in Cana takes the place in this Gospel of the Parable of the Bridegroom. In this miracle story, the best wine comes last, and it is not, I think, too fanciful to see in this the figure of the Christ and of the church, the "new Israel," the Lamb's bride. This testimony of John the Baptist to Jesus as the Lamb of God has its sequel in chapter 3, "He who has the bride is the bridegroom; the friend of the bridegroom, who stands and hears him, rejoices greatly at the bridegroom's voice" (vs. 29). Here we have the Bridegroom and the bride, the church.

As to the promise that Messiah is he who baptizes with the Holy Spirit, the Jewish apocalyptic literature is full of the notion that the Messianic Age will be one in which the Spirit of God is "poured out on all flesh." It will not be as before, when the Spirit of God came here or there, to this prophet or that; but all will prophesy. Remember how in Acts, Peter regards what has happened as a fulfillment of such an apocalyptic forecast (2:16-21). The Messiah is he who gathers the Messianic community, who are baptized with the Holy Spirit. It is not surprising, therefore, that the first chapter of this Gospel, after declaring the witness of John the Baptist that this is he who is the Lamb of God and who baptizes with the Holy Spirit, should go on to show Jesus beginning to gather the Messianic community (John 1:35-51), the church, or the "fellowship of the Holy Spirit," which is to do his will as he has come to do the Father's will. Andrew, Peter, Philip, and Nathanael, and presumably John, are called into this community.

Similarly, the cleansing of the temple, which is placed in this Gospel at the beginning of the ministry (John 2:13-22), is made the subject of an allegory or parable: "Destroy this temple, and in three days I will raise it up." The temple was built with hands (Mark 14:58); the temple of which he speaks would be built without hands. Here there seems to me to be an undoubted reference to the Pauline conception of the church as the temple of God.[8] It is the temple of his body of which he speaks, that body which is to be crucified, buried, and raised again and to manifest itself in his body, the church: "When therefore he was raised from the dead, his disciples remembered that he had said this; and they believed the scripture and the word which Jesus had spoken" (John 2:22). Thus is the church introduced to us in the very beginning of this Gospel, which, because it is about the Christ, is about the church.

In chapter three, we are introduced to the two kingdoms, sharply divided, of the world and of the

Spirit (John 3:1-21), with the necessity of the new birth for entry into the Kingdom of Spirit, where baptism is introduced (3:3-6). The Kingdom of the Spirit is made to depend on the Incarnation and the cross: "No one has ascended into heaven but he who descended from heaven" (John 3:13). "As Moses lifted up the serpent in the wilderness, so must the Son of man be lifted up, that whoever believes in him may have eternal life" (John 3:14-15). Both Jews and Samaritans may have this eternal life and drink the "living waters" (John 4:1-26). Later, Greeks are also admitted (John 12:20-26). The worship of the kingdom is "in spirit and truth" and is to be independent of Jewish or Samaritan shrines; it is to be universal (John 4:23). In chapter five, in the healing of the paralytic, we have a further indication of the character of those who are to be transformed and brought into the kingdom and of the kingdom's re-creating power in bringing such outcasts in.[9] Elsewhere, in healing stories, we have Jesus involved in the same controversies with the Jews which appear in the Synoptics, controversies about the Sabbath and about the class of people with whom he chooses to associate (John 9:1-41); but here the controversies have closer reference to the quarrel between church and synagogue.

The situation is not different from that of the Synoptics so far as the type whom Jesus calls into the church is concerned, the rejected and the outcasts.[10] This story of the healing of the paralytic is followed by the same contrast between the world and the church which we have noted before (John 5:19-29; cf. John 7:1-9), and the church is described as those who already have eternal life through the Resurrection of Jesus Christ (Paul's *arrhabōn*).

The biblical conception of the church as the "Israel of God," which we have seen in Paul and which finds expression elsewhere in the New Testament, is given in this Gospel in a new form in the discourse on the true seed of Abraham (John 8:31-59). The seed of Abraham is composed of the true believers, while others, although they have a lineal descent from Abraham, are the seed of the devil. In the same way that Paul gathers up the ancient Israelites into the church, through their baptism in the Red Sea, and their drinking of the same spiritual Rock as Christians, which Rock was Christ (1 Cor. 10:1-4), this writer gathers Abraham and his seed into the bosom of the church (John 8:36).[11] But all this has no meaning apart from the fact that Jesus is the eternal Word of God manifested in the flesh: "Before Abraham was, I am" (John 8:58).

In chapter ten we come to imagery which cannot be understood apart from the church—that of the Good Shepherd and his flock. It is rather startling that it finds expression in but three other places in the New Testament apart from the Gospels,[12] for it is such a familiar theme in the Old Testament. There can be little doubt that behind this chapter, at least two passages from the Old Testament are in the writer's mind —that of the good shepherd of Ezekiel (37:24) and that of the idle shepherd of Zechariah (11:16-17). It is the same contrast which is made here between the Good Shepherd and the hireling. In all this we must remember that to the Hebrew mind, there was little difference between shepherd and king.[18] Yahweh was the King of Israel and he was the Shepherd of Israel (Psalm 23). This familiar twenty-third psalm, which seems to us to carry an individualistic ring, did not necessarily carry the same individualistic ring to the Hebrew. Such Old Testament scholars as Gunkel, Gressmann, Mowinckel, Rowley, and Aubrey Johnson are inclined to interpret many of the apparently individualistic Psalms as expressive of the faith of Israel. The good king was the one who was shepherd to his people.[14] The Psalms are full of this idea and constantly set forth the ideal king as the one who follows God's rule, who is the king and shepherd of his people. Thus, to the Jew, the king and the shepherd represent what John Oman has described as "ultimate demand" and "ultimate succour."[15]

Here, in this chapter, these two ideas are not far apart and are brought to a focus in the notion that the Good Shepherd is the One who lays down his life for the sheep (John 10:11, 14). Note also that Jesus is not only the Good Shepherd, but he is the door of the sheepfold by which alone a man can enter. Furthermore, the Jew and the Gentile are together in the "one flock" (John 10:16). Here, all that we have about the reconciliation of the Jew and Gentile in the fellowship of the church in such Pauline passages as Ephesians, chapter 2, is summed up: "I have other sheep, that are not of this fold; I must bring them also, and they will heed my voice. So there shall be one flock, one shepherd."[16] The close connection of all this with the "suffering servant" of Second Isaiah is obvious: "He will feed his flock like a shepherd, he will gather the lambs into his arm, and carry them in his bosom, and will gently lead those that have their young" (40:11).[17] Here, too, we have the parallel of the Johannine Gospel to the Parable of the Lost Sheep (Luke 15:3-7); but here the corporate idea is more closely expressed: there is one Shepherd and one flock. Note also the constant reference to the fact that the sheep *know* the voice of the Shepherd, that the Shepherd knows the sheep and they know him. Again, this knowledge is likened to the knowledge which the Father and the Son have of each other (John 10:4, 14-15). We must remember that the writer uses the word "know," not of abstract analytical knowledge, but of intimate personal knowledge. The church is the true *koinōnia*, in which there is interpenetration of personality without loss of personal distinctiveness; it reflects, however feebly, the real structure of reality.

The close connection of the Eucharist with all this is seen in the discourse after the feeding miracle (John, chap. 6), and in the discourses in the Upper Room, which in this Gospel take the place of the institution of the Lord's Supper (chaps. 13-14). Already, in Mark's Gospel, the feeding miracle has sacramental and eschatological significance, especially the feeding of the four thousand (Mark 6:34-42; 8:1-10). In John, chapter 6, Jesus claims to be "the living bread which came down from heaven" (vs. 51); he is "the true bread from heaven," which God gives (vs. 32). As with Paul, in 1 Corinthians, chapter 10, this bread is contrasted with the manna in the wilderness, as the bread which gives eternal life (John 6:32-40). Continually the feeding on this bread is made to depend on eating his flesh and drinking his blood (John 6:

53-56), and though this is explained as something spiritual (vss. 62-63), it is none the less accepted as something realistic. To eat the flesh and to drink the blood of Christ is the same thing as believing that Jesus has come from God (John 6:64) and to be among the true disciples who confess that in him are the words of eternal life (vs. 68). It is to be one with Christ and with those who are with him.

The spiritual meaning of all this, on its corporate side, is elaborated in the actions and discourses in the Upper Room. The washing of the disciples' feet shows the spirit in which all service for Christ must be undertaken, and in which all rule in his kingdom must be exercised. The poignancy of his grief is shown by the fact that at the Last Supper, a traitor sat at table with the fellowship group. It was his "own familiar friend" that was set to do the dastardly deed which broke fellowship. No wonder the writer says, "So, after receiving the morsel, he immediately went out; *and it was night*" (John 13:30). It was black night in the heart of Judas, and it was night with that loyal band where fellowship had been so ruthlessly broken for thirty pieces of silver.

Then begins at 13:31 and continuing to 17:26, what might be called "The Apocalypse of the Holy Spirit." This is the Gospel's counterpart to the Pentecost of

Acts, chapters 1 and 2. He tells of his "going away" and of his "coming again" in his "other self," the Paraclete, who is to comfort the church and guide into all truth (John 16:13) and convict the world of sin, of righteousness, and of judgment to come (16:8-11). His "going away" includes his death, his resurrection, and his ascension, and is spoken of as his glorification (John 13:31). Just as Jesus has revealed God, so that it can be said, "He who has seen me has seen the Father" (John 14:9), so the Holy Spirit is to take the things of Christ and show them to the church (John 16:13-14). It is expedient for the disciples that Jesus should go away (John 16:7) for, in his going away, he, who has been localized, would be universalized in time and space in the coming of the Holy Spirit and in the life of the Spirit-filled community. As the world had hated Jesus, so it will hate the church (John 15:18), which is chosen out of the world; and it will hate the church because, though still in it, it is not of it (vs. 19). In the world, the church is destined for tribulation, but he has already overcome the world (John 16:33). The final issue of the struggle is not uncertain, for the church already has the *eschaton* in the victory of "powerless power" which Jesus achieves in the cross and the Resurrection. The church will ever be the church militant, but she is already, in an eschatological sense, the church triumphant. This is all brought to a focus in chapter sixteen, which repeats in a double way three themes:

1. The persecuted church, 1-4.
2. The glorified Lord, 5-6.
3. The coming of the Comforter, 7-13.

\* \* \* \* \* \* \*

3. The work of the Comforter, 14-16.
2. The glorified Lord, 16-31.
1. The persecuted church, 32-33.

The close connection of Christ and the church is obvious. What happened to him, happens to the church. He is crucified, dead, buried, risen, ascended and glorified; the church is crucified, dead, buried, risen, ascended and glorified in him—*symbolically*, in baptism, as each member is called out of the world into him, and as the church corporately, in the Eucharist, shares in his flesh and blood and at the same time is joined to the seraphic choir above; and *really*, in the life of the church in the world as it manifests his spirit and shows him forth to the world.

In the midst of these discourses in the Upper Room, which all center on the new commandment of *agapē* (John 15:9-12), comes the allegory of the vine (vss.

1-8). We have already seen that Israel was regarded as God's vineyard (see p. 68). In the Maccabean period, coins were struck with Israel represented as the vine of God. In the Testament of Levi (chap. 2), the Messiah, as the true Israel, is called the Vine and, similarly, in the Apocalypse of Baruch. Here, in Jesus as the True Vine, we have the same "identity with difference" between Christ and the church that we have in Paul's "body of Christ" (see pp. 69ff.). Note that Jesus is "the Vine," the whole vine, including the branches. He is not the stock and roots, with the branches attached; he is the Vine itself including the pruned branches and those that bear no fruit, so intimate is the relationship between Jesus and those whom he gathers to himself. This intimacy is explained (John 15:9-27) as being, not theosophical but *personal*, as belonging to the realm of personal understanding and loyalty; and this, which is a mystical reality, is a far greater mystery than any theosophic union. Those who are within this corporate relationship are his *friends*, who know the innermost secrets of his heart, as he does of the Father's (John 15:14-15). Such union results in *doing* his will as he does the will of the Father. There can be no real union without this.[18] Again we have the "identity with difference" emphasized in that, as he was persecuted, so the church will be persecuted for his sake (John 15:20-21); as he was persecuted for bearing witness of the Father, so they will be persecuted for bearing witness of Christ; as the Holy Spirit will bear witness of Christ, so the church, represented here by the apostles, will bear witness of Christ, will identify itself with him (John 15:26-27).

The discourses in the Upper Room come to a climax in the high priestly prayer in chapter seventeen, which is a prayer for the faithfulness of the church, faithfulness not only to the spirit of Jesus, the spirit of love, but also to the truth of the Incarnation (John 17:8). Here the true corporeity of the church is emphasized and explained. His followers are to be one, as he and the Father are one (John 17:11, 21). That unity which there is between Father and Son in the one Godhead, which is not the unity of mystical absorption but of separation of Persons united in one will, is to characterize the church. What meaning this prayer must have had for the writer in a day when the unity of the church was being seriously threatened by Docetic teachers! The world will be able to receive the truth of the Incarnation only if this unity is manifested (John 17:21). Again, there is the closest identity of the Christ and the church. The glory which the Father has given the Son, the Son has given the church (John 17:22). The church is in Christ, and Christ is in the church, as the Father is in Christ

(John 17:23). It is made quite clear that the church is to continue as a historical reality: "I do not pray that thou shouldst take them out of the world, but that thou shouldst keep them from the evil one" (John 17:15). Behind this petition one can sense the poignant longing of the church of the writer's day, no doubt intensified by the delayed Parousia and the imminent Domitian persecution—a longing for some other way of securing the redemptive process than by suffering and witnessing for Christ, namely, by translation.[19] Like the Lord, the church is not of the world (John 17:16; 18:36), but it is sent into the world as he was sent into it by the Father (17:18). Christians corporately also have an Incarnation—a visible manifest form—and they are apostolic in that they are the "sent ones." Of his apostleship they were convinced—the Father had *sent* him (John 17:25)[20] —and now they have an apostleship and a mission in the world, involving the same suffering and the same glory. There can be no escape here from the concept of the church as integral to the gospel, the "good news" in Christ Jesus.

The Gospel of John is echoed in the First Epistle of John, where the unity of the church in *agapē*, which is not a sentiment, but an active self-giving impulse, is stressed as over against the loveless attitude of superior gnostic-minded individuals who threaten the corporate fellowship and seek to undermine the concrete reality of the Incarnation and of the church as a historical reality continuing that Incarnation. The church, declares the writer, is not an aggregation of superior, sophisticated persons who regard with disdain those of inferior intellectual equipment, proud in their pseudophilosophical grasp of abstract theosophical notions; rather, it is a fellowship of those who have faith in Christ, who was manifested *in the flesh*, and who themselves, by his grace, manifest the love to one another wherewith God loved them. Again and again the humility of the true believers is stressed by their being called "little children" (1 John 2:1, 12, 28; 3:7, 18; 4:4; 5:21), a phrase also found in the Gospel (John 13:33). There is the same contrast between the world and the church (1 John, chap. 3), and the world hates the church because of its witness to Christ. Similarly, we have the same emphasis on Christ's abiding in the church and the church's abiding in Christ (1 John 2:28; 4:13); and, as in Paul, the members of the church are "the children of God" (1 John 3:1).

Here, then, is a picture of the church set in the Hellenic world, a world seething with ideas, many of which were antithetic to historical reality, pursuing its mission of witnessing to the "good news" of the Incarnation, something which had happened in a particular place and at a particular time, as God's redemptive act, an act which involved that the Christ *be made flesh*, the concretion of the Absolute. "That the Christian faith is thus rooted in the concrete, the actual, the historical, has been a constant theme all through the epistle."[21] It is only with this safe and sure foundation that we can mount up to heaven and know that "it is at the same time concerned with the suprahistorical, the eternal, the ultimately real."[22] The safeguard against the airy speculations of the gnostic-minded superior people is "to live within the fellowship of the Church, and to adhere loyally and with understanding to the authentic tradition of the apostles; keeping always in view that which the apostles attest, and which creates the fellowship of the Church —the historical revelation of God in the life and words of Jesus Christ. To put it briefly for our own situation: a concentration upon the New Testament, and the Gospels in particular, in the context of a living Church fellowship, is our best safeguard against modern idolatries."*

---

*C. H. Dodd, *The Johannine Epistles*, p. 142. Moffatt New Testament Commentary series. Used by permission of Hodder & Stoughton, Harper & Brothers, and Professor Dodd.

# V

## THE NATURE OF THE CHURCH

As WE have seen, it is no mere figure of speech when Paul names the church the "body of Christ"—it is a mystical reality. The church is that concrete reality by which Christ becomes manifest to the world, and by which he acts in history. It is the "dwelling place of God in the Spirit." Wherever the church of Christ is, at that point the eternal penetrates (shoots down into) the temporal. We have also seen that Paul went even further in the language which he dared to use. More than once he suggests that "the Christ" is not simply the historic Jesus, nor even the glorified Christ, but the glorified Christ plus the church. It is this daring identification of the Christ and the church which underlies his discourses on Christian marriage in Ephesians: the church is the bride of the Christ, and we are members of his body—"of his body, of his flesh, and of his bones," according to one corrupt text (Eph. 5:30, A.V.). We have seen that it underlies, too, his amazing statement in Colossians: "Now I rejoice in my sufferings for your sake, and in my flesh complete what remains of Christ's afflictions for the sake of his body, that is, the church"

(1:24). How can anyone say such things without blasphemy, unless he speaks from an experience of *fellowship* so real and so close that it involves that interpenetration of personality which is the hidden secret of reality? We have also seen that this was understood by Paul in his earlier Corinthian correspondence, where we have explicitly the boldest of all his assertions about the Christ (1 Cor. 12:12). There he definitely calls the church the Christ: "For just as the body [the physical body] is one and has many members, and all the members of the body, though many, are one body, *so it is with Christ.*" Here, following his argument, we should expect to find, "so it is with the church"; and, indeed, that is what he means, as the subsequent argument shows. His substitution of "the Christ" for "the church" is not accidental. It is intentional—Christ and the church are, in some sense, identified.

We have seen that the same doctrine of the church runs through the Fourth Gospel, where the church is set forth as the universalizing of "the Word made flesh." It is expedient that Jesus should go away, so that the Paraclete may come (John 16:7). But the Paraclete is, in a way, Jesus' "other self": " 'A little while, and you will see me no more; again a little while, and you will see me' " (John 16:16). He is going away a little while only that his witness, which had been necessarily circumscribed by temporality and locality, might be universalized in the church, which was to be catholic—in all ages and in all places. The church is the continuation of the Incarnation, if we mean by "Incarnation," not only his being made flesh, but all that that involves—his death, burial, resurrection, ascension and exaltation, and his sending of the Holy Spirit. But, more than that, it is the continuation of that process which began with the Word in the world, and continued with the Word in Israel and in the "true Israel," and reached the limit of concretion in a once-for-all event in Jesus of Nazareth, the "Word made flesh." From that point, there is a widening out again—the fellowship grows, breaking the limits of time and space, and perpetuates itself within history in a living institutional form, so that it never becomes coterminous with the whole human race. In truth, it is the "little flock," the "leaven," which leavens the world, the "salt of the earth," which preserves the world.[1] It is that point in history where God in Christ is floodlighted through his Spirit. In reality, the church is Christ manifest in the flesh, as Jesus of Nazareth was God manifest in the flesh.

We have seen, further, that all this cannot be taken as the theologizing of a Paul nor the philosophizing of a John. It is implicit in all the showing forth of God in the Old Testament from the time that Abra-

ham "went out, not knowing where he was to go."
We catch the authentic accents of it in the words about
the "suffering servant" and the "Son of man." We
see it in the action of Jesus in choosing the apostles
"to be with him" and finally *sending* them as he had
been *sent* by the Father.[2] And we meet it in the primitive church. Luke gives the clue in the opening verses
of his prologue to the Acts: "In the first book, O
Theophilus, I have dealt with all that Jesus *began* to
do and teach." The earthly life of Jesus was only
the *beginning* of his doing and teaching. The impli-
cation is that in the second book there is to be an account of "all that Jesus *continued* to do and teach."
Notice, also, that *doing* is as important as *teaching*.
The word is not primarily a spoken word. Remember, too, how Peter declared that *he* had not healed
the lame man, but that Jesus had done it. The church
began her life with the undeniable conviction that
Jesus was alive, and that he was showing himself to
the world in the "beloved community." Such was
the church's conviction then, and such must be her
conviction now.

The church differs, therefore, from every other
society in the world. All other institutions, as compared with her, are of human contriving and are
mortal. They have their beginnings, though those
beginnings may be lost in obscurity; and they come to

a definite end. This is true even of such institutions as empires, nations, and civilizations.[3] But the church is not of human contriving—it is divine. It has ontological reality. Neither is it mortal—it is immortal: "On this rock I will build my church, and the powers of death shall not prevail against it." "Lo, I am with you always, to the close of the age." The church represents that point in the creative and redemptive activity of God where he is revealed; and as such it is a continuation of that process of his showing forth of himself which was begun when the Word "was in the world, . . . yet the world knew him not." The church is a supernatural society within a natural environment—"a colony of heaven," as Paul called it.[4]

If the church is the perpetuation of the Incarnation, it will have about it those paradoxical qualities in duality which he, our Lord, had. Like him, it is both human and divine. In him, we recognize "two natures in one Person," to use the language of Chalcedon. In the church, there are "two natures in one body," and it is essential that we do not forget this. Where there is concretion, there is always this paradoxical duality. The fact that the church is human is clear enough—how terribly human she is at times! But the church is also divine and not a mere human society. Like Christ, the church is temporal and eternal—the church militant and the church triumphant.

It is never just the church at any single time point in history. It includes the apostles, prophets, martyrs, saints of all ages, and presumably our Lord himself as the Head. Like him, it is local and yet universal. It is never just the community in a single locality. When a body of people, say twenty, are gathered together as *a* church to offer to God the sacrifice of praise and thanksgiving, they are joined to the whole church in time and space. Like him, it is in the world, but not of it. To the outsider, it may appear like any other community in the world; but it is a different order from the world order, inspired by a different motive. That is why it does not assume political shape and knows no barriers of race or nation, and why it is motivated by a different motive from that of political expediency—the motive of love. Like him, it is weak and yet all-powerful. So often, and perhaps never so much as at the present time, the church appears weak and ineffective; but there is a sense in which we need never tremble for the ark of God: the gates of Hades do not prevail against her, however the contrary may seem to be the case. The church is unconquerable, as we have seen in Germany and in Russia, though there is no need to see this complacently. Apathy is a far greater danger to the church than opposition, and the church is perhaps never so much the "true church" as when she is the "suffering church."

Like him, the church is fallible[5] and infallible. This may be strong meat for Protestants, but we must look at it fairly and squarely.

Catholics of the Latin type[6] have greatly erred—at least in theory—in asserting that general councils do not err, and in framing a rigid, logical, and mechanical theory of infallibility, necessitating eventually a single organ of infallibility. But Protestants have equally erred in denying the infallibility of the church. The church is *both* fallible and infallible. It is this "either/or" policy which has prevented much true understanding of the nature of the church and, indeed, of reality as such. Where there is concreteness and process, there must be this paradoxical duality. It is especially the characteristic of all livingness. The church is the "carrier of possibilities,"[7] which in her life and witness become actualized so that her rectitude, unlike that of any other society, is invested with infinite importance. No doubt it is in the "crisis act," in the apocalyptic realm, that the church is seen most clearly as infallible—that an "eternal now" is given in the movement of time. The infallibility of the church is, therefore, to be looked for in its religious (apocalyptic) attitudes and ethical temper, rather than in mystical forms. There is no clear-cut logical way of determining an infallible utterance of the church. We may quote the document referred to at the beginning of this paragraph: "The Orthodox Church gives its dogmatic judgments by the action of the Holy Spirit in various ways, but always in ways of Church *sobornost* [ecumenicity and fellowship life]. Sometimes these judgments are arrived at by long and stormy discussion [the Christological disputes] and are consummated by a solemn definition of the faith in ecumenical or local councils, accepted by the Church as the words of truth, and sometimes rejected [as in the case of the false councils]; or else *tacite consensu* by the life of the Church itself." The judgment of history has often to be pronounced before we can become aware that the church has spoken by word or *action* (and often action is the more important) an infallible word of God. More recently this has been witnessed to in history in Russia and in Germany. No one can doubt that in these two countries the church uttered a "sure word of God." To believe that the word of the church, given in its life and witness, when the church acts like a church under the judgment of the word of God, and submitting herself to the guidance of the Holy Spirit—to believe that that word is just like the word of any other corporation is to deny the divinity of the church. It was a Disciple of Christ who said in 1888: "There is a tendency among Protestants to disregard the authority of the church, and so to look upon it simply as a moral society. The Disciples believe the church divine, and that it is as important to obey the bride as the bridegroom. Hence they do not believe that a man can be a Christian outside of the church."[8] This is a strong statement and sounds like one made by a Catholic, even a Roman Catholic, but it was written by a Disciple and evidently represented the Disciple witness at that time. We need to remind ourselves of it.

We turn to another question, that of the church universal and the local church. This is involved in the deeper question of the nature of the church and involves the more practical question of church polity, with which I am not particularly concerned in this book. The word *ecclēsia* is found no less than one hundred and fifteen times in the New Testament, and in all but three of these it refers to the church, either local or universal.[9] In seventy-nine of these it is used of the local church, either in the singular or plural; in twenty-seven it is used of the church universal; in six cases it is doubtful whether the local church or the church universal is intended. To the twenty-seven cases where *ecclēsia* is used of the church universal, must be added twenty uses of the expression "body of Christ," three references to the church as the "Israel of God," and a number of instances of such expressions as "the household of faith," "a people for God's own possession," and "the saints," which have reference to the church universal. At first, the church universal is the local church. But this does not mean that the local church is before the church universal, as we have seen (see pp. 60f.). The word *ecclēsia* appears to have been first used of the one church and later applied to the local church as an outcrop of the one church in that locality, whether it was a city church, a house church, or the church of an area. There is always the tension between the local church and the one church, just as there is the tension between the individual member and the corporate body in the local church. Each local church, while expressing the one faith, having the same rite of initiation and the same definitive form of worship, the Eucharist, and pursuing the same way of life, nevertheless has its own individuality. Just as in the Godhead, there is a distinction of Persons in Father, Son, and Holy Spirit, and yet one God, so in the local church, there is a distinction between one member and another, and yet one corporate society; and in the one church, there is a distinction between one local expression of it and another, and yet one body. It is not mystical absorption, but "identity with difference."[10]

We must remember that in the period covered by the New Testament, there was apostolic oversight in the local churches and, whatever there was of congregational autonomy, there was nothing of absolute independency. Further, there does not seem to have been more than one church in one city, however many house congregations there may have been. These churches appear to have been under the immediate oversight of the city presbytery. In districts, there was the closest cooperation between town churches, as witness Galatia. Mother churches also seem to have had some pre-eminence, though not jurisdiction, from earliest times.[11] While among the churches there were no doubt differences of usage and custom, there was a fundamental unity and certainly a unity in faith and sacraments as well as in ethical life. Throughout his mission, we see Paul striving to keep this unity. He made his churches imitators of the churches which were in Judea (1 Thess. 2:14). The Jerusalem Conference is another example of the same thing (Acts, chap. 15). The catholic church could be recognized wherever it went.

What then is the function of the church? The church is in the world to redeem it. In her life and witness she continues that work which was begun and, in an eschatological sense, completed in the Incarnate Lord. She has the double task of adding to her own number, as the "ark of salvation," and of transforming the world, as the "bringer of salvation." In this second task, she is the "powerhouse" from which spiritual power goes out into the world. In her possession she has the "good news" by which she brings in those who are "added to her"; but she has also the "good life," contained in what Archbishop Temple called the "middle axioms," by which she transforms the world in which she lives her life.

How does the church put into practice these "middle axioms" which are a part of her heritage? How is the ideal translated into the practical? This is by no means such a simple problem as it has sometimes been conceived to be, both by Christians and by critics of the church. The fact is that every Christian lives his life under two loyalties: (*a*) loyalty to God as revealed in Jesus Christ; (*b*) loyalty to the state in which he lives. The first of these loyalties is, or should be, the same for every Christian. But the second is not, a fact which raises complex political and ethical problems. Between these two loyalties there is always a tension. This tension varies according to: (*a*) the measure in which the state expresses the Christian ethic in its political, economic, and social life; (*b*) the depth of apprehension of the will of God in the Christian himself. Sub-Christian conduct on the part of a Christian or of a local or territorial church may, therefore, be due to two causes: (*a*) imperfect apprehension of the Christian standard; (*b*) refusal to resist the state, even though recognizing its demands to be sub-Christian, or even anti-Christian.

Paul, in Romans, chapter 13, I think, sees the matter as too simple. The state is ordained by the providence of God to secure order and justice, which are necessary for the existence of the church's ordered life. Otherwise, anarchy and lawlessness would threaten the life of the Christian community. Law and order are necessary conditions of its existence, and the state is ordained of God to secure these by force. But this is too simple a solution of a more complex problem. And Paul himself was executed by the same state (now become corrupt under the rule of Nero) for refusing to obey its requirements, and before the century is out, another Christian writer could speak of it as "Babylon the great, mother of harlots" and as "the beast" (Rev. 17:5; cf. 14:8; 18:2, 10, 21). This has been illustrated in our own time by the fact that from 1933 onward, many sincere Christians, who endorsed Paul's words with reference to the British State, did at the same time urge upon German Christians the very opposite attitude toward the German State. On the other hand, if we say, as some Christians do, that the state is wholly evil, that it has gone to the devil and that the church must have nothing to do with it, that it must sink into what a Roman statesman of the second century called "desperate inactivity," this also is too simple. To say nothing further, such an attitude is a historical impossibility. Christians, as

[ 111 ]

well as other people, are unable to withdraw themselves from responsibility for the state. Christians are in the world, like all other folk, though they may not be of it.

To think of the state simply as either wholly good or as wholly evil is misleading. The state itself has a mysterious dual nature. There is in it, as Paul saw, an element of righteousness, creating law and order. But there is also in it a demonic element, a principle of evil which works against its own health. The first element is there, however corrupt the state may be; and it is never to be forgotten that the second element is there, however exalted and advanced the state may be. In the Christian's and the church's relationship to the state, we are often faced, not with a choice between an absolute good and an absolute evil, but between two evils, one of which is relatively good. The problem often is one of doing evil that good may come; and, further, so complex is the situation that the good sought often turns out to be a worse evil than the evil overcome—calamity comes just the same. This is the human dilemma, the dilemma of historicity, which arises from the fact that the *concrete* situation is never *ideal*.

This means that we must recognize the difference between the *ideal* and the *practical*. Let me illustrate this simply by showing, in one instance of a practical situation, the impossibility of completely fulfilling the ideal expressed in the golden rule, "Do unto others as you would that they should do to you." A train is standing in a country station. It is due to start. But there is a number of workmen running up the line to catch the train. The stationmaster sees them. What is he to do? Must he start the train on time and leave the men behind? Or must he delay the train and allow the men to catch it? Besides his own duty to start the train on time, other issues are involved. There are passengers on the train who, some miles on, are to make a connection with an express which will land them in a distant city. It is vital to them that they make their connection. Now it is obvious that if the stationmaster wants to do to the men as he would be done by, he must delay the train. But, on the other hand, if the men running up the line want to do to the stationmaster as they would be done by, they will wish him to start the train on time. The train itself cannot fulfill both behests. Not all situations with which we are faced are of this kind, but the important thing is that there are such situations which arise from the fact that we are involved in the mesh of historicity.

This brings us to the point that in all practical issues, we have to recognize two kinds of compromise. The first I shall call "deliberate compromise." This occurs when two alternatives are open to us, each of which is possible. For instance, a man may be asked to practice something shady in business. He has the alternative of acceptance or refusal. It may be refusal at serious cost to himself; nevertheless, refusal is possible. The second I shall call "inevitable compromise," and it is just this kind of compromise which is often involved in the church's relationship to the state.

The pacifist is a good example. Once his country has gone to war, in countries like ours, where pacifists are not executed, he is inevitably involved in compromise. He cannot escape it; he can only determine where he will draw the line. Some accept noncombatant service in the armed forces; some, further back, accept such service only in the unarmed forces; some, further back still, refusing any kind of alternative service, refuse even to pay income tax; many go to prison. But, even so, they are involved in the war situation so long as they continue to live, to use food and clothing, to be dependent on money. Taking some lines of resistance to war may even involve the pacifist indirectly in assisting the enemy, when he has no desire to do so. In such a situation the pacifist has mainly to content himself with being something, rather than with doing something; and it must be remembered that *this itself is an important thing,* as it is important that such a witness *be kept alive.* Even our

Lord, in his historical existence, was subject to "inevitable compromise." He was a member of what was virtually an "occupied country," which had its political party of "partisans," as it had its "collaborators" and "quislings." He was a member of none of these parties. But, although the occupying government was based on principles contrary to those he proclaimed, nevertheless, to do his work, he had to be dependent on this government. To ignore "inevitable compromise" is to sink into unreality, and any criticism of the church which fails to take account of it is unsound. But this "inevitable compromise" is there to be *overcome* by the church, not to be accepted complacently. Always there is the "church within the church," bearing witness in her own heroic life to some "absolute" which must be translated into the concrete realities of history. The church in her divine nature has that within her which, if her witness remains true, transcends the historical relativities of our life. She is in the world, not to conform to the world, but to redeem it.

I hope by now that three things are clear about the church's way of action:

1. It is clear that the church herself cannot take political shape and become another political entity over against the state. Our Lord refused to identify his kingdom with such a political entity. For the

church to do so would be to deny her nature as "a colony of heaven."[12] *It is the political irrelevancy of the church which constitutes her political power.* She is a "powerhouse," a "leaven" within the whole of society. She cannot therefore be the Republican party, the Democratic party, the Labor party, or even the Christian party at prayer.[13]

2. It is also clear that the church cannot take national shape.[14] She cannot become the handmaid of the nation to serve her national pride. This also would be to deny her true nature, for she is catholic, or universal, including both Jew and Gentile. This is a deeper question than that of an established church versus a free church. A free church may be as national or more so in her attitude than an established church.[15]

3. It is further clear that the church has to struggle for a Christian civilization, which it must be recognized is something quite different from the life of the church herself. A Christian civilization may be described as one in which the main principles of the Christian ethic are actualized, and in which Christians themselves are able to take on the full disciplines of the Christian life without interference from the state. The church must struggle to see Christian principles embodied in civilization, at whatever cost to herself or to the particular nation in which she is domiciled.

[ 116 ]

Today we are "between the times." One age, that of Christendom and its surviving Christian civilization, is in its death throes, and another is struggling to be born. What shape this new age will take is still uncertain. We do know that a serious bid is being made to establish the "secular state," and in some places we have seen the state assume totalitarian form of one kind or another. The doctrine of the omnicompetence of the state, with its consequence that the individual and all institutions, from the family to the church, exist for the state, and for the state alone, has in places assumed violent form. Even where democracy holds good, as in our own countries, there are forces at work which threaten to lead to a more rigid control of public opinion and to the disappearance of religious freedom. In such a situation, the problem of church and state is no longer the *legal* problem of established versus free church, but the more vital problem of God versus Caesar. The very existence of the church as a free corporation may be threatened.

Archbishop Temple (father of the late archbishop) could say, "Force is entrusted to the State in order that the State may prevent lawless force." But this is altogether too benign an attitude for our situation. Much of the good that the state seeks, it seeks through power; and the church knows that the greatest good is beyond power and force and that the greatest evil reveals itself through power. And this remains fully true, even though the evil which power includes may be a necessary evil, creating order and combating disorder. There is a very real sense in which the state does not "bear the sword in vain." But we must remember that even throughout its legitimate activity of creating order, the destructive tendency of political power remains real and living. For this reason the church must realize that the ideal order of perfect justice can never be realized in the sphere of the state by political means.[16] Only by the transfiguration of the world into the Kingdom of God, which is love (powerless power), can the final solution be achieved. The church has this in anticipation in her *fellowship* life, her free community of love. Already she has tasted of the powers of the age to come. It is this which makes her the *leaven* in society.[17]

It is this character of the church as leaven which makes it essential that she work in the world apocalyptically, a word which carries the meanings of revelatory, catastrophically, and personally. This, at one and the same time, causes her to disbelieve in straight-line progress and in pessimistic despair. She is in the world to redeem it. Her position is not one of privilege, but of responsibility. That she is described as "leaven" means that she is a hidden explosive force, for leaven in its operation is both unseen and explosive. As history moves on, doors open and shut. In God's providence, some open which "no man can shut," and others shut which "no man can open." The "day of visitation" passes, and we have failed "to know our peace." The straight-line progress enthusiasts spend a deal of time trying to batter down doors which can never be opened at that precise moment, trying to "force the hand of God"; while those who are set for the *status quo* often prevent our entering doors which are standing wide open, inviting entrance. History knows both progress and regress, as opportunities are taken or rejected. It knows both evolution and devolution, and often because it rejects *involution*. The judgments of God are as certain as his mercies. In the "crisis hour," the "ripe time," the "fulfilled time," there appears the "tide in the affairs of men, which, taken at the flood, leads on to fortune; omitted, all the voyage of their lives is bound in shallows and in miseries."[18] In such "crisis moments," if we know "the things that make for peace," a relative situation is transcended, so that an ethical question which was once relevant becomes wholly irrelevant.

There is always the world, and there is always the church in the world, living her life at the level of "inevitable compromise," the compromise of historicity.[19] But there is also always the "church within the church," not in the sense of denominations, but in the sense of "pockets," which express an "absolute good," either a "pure absolute" or a "partial absolute," expressing some element in the Christian ethic not yet realized in society nor in the life of the whole church. When the "ripe time" comes, these "absolutes" may expand so as to take in the whole world as well as the whole church. A good example of this process is the abolition of the slave trade and of slavery in the British Empire. No one will deny that the impetus for this came from the church, newly awakened by the Evangelical Revival. It was not only a social question, but a political and economic one. The end, in July, 1833, came with apocalyptic suddenness. At first, the small group of enthusiasts were regarded, even by many of their fellow Christians, as little other than dreamers and fanatics. Even those within the group were not wholly optimistic of success when success was imminent. As William Wilberforce lay dying in London, Thomas Fowell Buxton was shepherding through Parliament the bill which was to emancipate 700,000 slaves in the British Dominions at a cost of £20,000,000 to the National Exchequer, no small sum in those days. Against terrific opposition and indifference, some of it from within the church, the bill passed; and within a few years what had previously been a burning question—Could a Christian be a slave-owner?—had become a purely academic one and wholly irrelevant within the living situation.

In this way the church maintains her witness against social, political, and economic evils. She is the carrier of possibilities which first become actualized in her own life and then in the life of society. The true church is always the church courageously facing the *future*, refusing to be satisfied with the *status quo*, dynamic in her life and in her influence; and she dares to face the future so courageously because she *is so deeply rooted in the past*, unlike many rootless and doctrinaire systems which are offered the suffering masses as husks for bread. In her bosom she carries eternity, into which are gathered the past, present, and future.

# VI

## THE DIVINE-HUMAN RELATIONSHIP
## IN THE CHURCH

T HE question arises, How is the relationship between the divine and the human realized within the church? There are three possible kinds of relationships between persons—mechanical, legal or transactional, and true personal relationships. In the first two of these, the narrow logic of the schools holds good. They are what in mathematics we call "one-one" relationships. In the third, this logic is never completely adequate to the field.

Is the church mechanically controlled by God? Is God working in her by might and omnipotence? We are not questioning God's omnipotence, which is a fact not to be ignored; rather, we are asking, What way has he *chosen* to work in the church? It can hardly be denied that when attention has been exclusively concentrated on might and omnipotence, it has often led to theosophic and occult notions, creating an atmosphere in which Christian mysticism has developed a nonpersonal and almost pantheistic type, and morality has found it more and more difficult to secure a foothold. To think of God as being limited to this way of working is surely a contradiction of Christian theology.[1]

Again, is the church legally controlled? Is she under orders? There can be no doubt that the church is under orders. As a divine reality she has a "form" into which to grow up. Her life is not to be controlled by human caprice, nor is it to be subject to the fickleness of the human will. But the deeper question must be asked, Is the One who issues the orders in *legal* relationship to the church or in a relationship similar to that of a father to his family? This makes a world of difference to the *spirit* in which orders will be obeyed or defied. Both in the old Israel and in the new Israel the spirit of legalism has done much damage, though nothing like the damage which has been done by the easygoing sentimentalism which has chosen to ignore the awful holiness of God. So often this attitude has concentrated on mercy and pity to the exclusion of righteousness. Nevertheless, a mere legalism is likely to produce religious practices which, instead of being disciplines, are of the nature of merit-making devices. Such legalism often also implies a rigid doctrine of infallibility, either of the church or of Holy Scripture, or of both, bound up with traditional words and practices, which leaves no room for the witness of God in the present historical form of the church (see pp. 105ff). I have in mind, here, the damage which has often been done in theology and in the life of the church by the rigid theory of the verbal inspiration of Holy Scripture, which is no invention of Protestantism, but which was a controlling idea in the medieval church. This, in the course of the ages, resulted in a *legalistic* and *abstract* system of doctrine, often quite unrelated to real life. When applied to the doctrines of grace and of justification, this could do no other than lead to the medieval system of penance, with merit-making works of supererogation as its corollary. In modern times it has worked havoc in Protestantism in producing a number of sects which conceive of the New Testament as a kind of blueprint, detailing the precise forms of Christian belief and practice. Above all, such an overemphasis of legal relationship can give no hope of fellowship,[2] no possibility of our really being sons of God. Finally, to think of God's relationship to the church in merely legal terms fails to allow for the revelation of God in Christ.

According to the revelation of God in Christ, God is in *personal* relationship to the church; the church is *personally* directed and inspired. This is a much more difficult thing for us to bear and involves on God's part a great deal more patience than we are sometimes prepared to allow for. The problem of God's grace, of his active love, is a problem which can have no solution in the realm of mechanical or of legal relationship. If we think of God's dealing with us as personal, as a father deals with his children, we cannot neatly weigh out what is *given* and what is *received;* what is of grace and what of merit.

It is true that when we are speaking of God, the parallel between father and child is never completely adequate. But, if God has *chosen* so to relate himself to his people, this condescension on his part is also of his grace, and it means that God himself has chosen not to *possess* and *overcome* persons, but rather to win them by his love. God's gifts do not suborn men and women, as ours may often do; for God's gifts are really the giving of himself. He does not by his giving rob us of our most precious possession—that of being persons, of being ourselves, which is also his gift to us.[3] We must go deeper and realize, as Oman says, that "we are nothing except what we receive, and yet we can receive nothing to profit except as our own.'" To stress *love* rather than *law* does not mean the lessening of moral responsibility, but its heightening. What it does mean, is that absolute religious dependence and the freedon of moral responsibility go hand in hand.

Moreover, in a love relationship, which is what a true personal relationship is, there can be no question of merit making. Here we are in a relationship where such things are transcended. Again, in a love relationship, we transcend mere justice—in fact, justice is not a characteristic Christian virtue at all, but a pagan one. To offend against law may be serious, or it may not be serious; but to traduce a loyalty, to break the heart of love, is despicable. Finally, in a true personal relationship, the whole legal phraseology of bondage and freedom is transcended; for, in a love relationship, he who is most loyal is most free. That is why Paul could speak of the perfect liberty of those who are in Christ Jesus, and why George Matheson could write:

> Make me a captive, Lord,
> And then I shall be free;
> Force me to render up my sword,
> And I shall conqueror be.

And that is why Benjamin Waugh could sing:

> Lord, it is coming to ourselves
> When thus we come to Thee;
> The bondage of Thy loveliness
> Is perfect liberty.

This is not sentimental hymn writing; it is the description of reality as it is revealed in the mystery that God is love.

In a church personally related to God, the demand is made that we should not be God's spoiled children. Our faith in God springs from, and is measured by, his faith in us: "We love, because he first loved us" (1 John 4:19; see also vs. 10). This is the characteristic biblical way of looking at the matter, and we often fail to understand how topsy-turvy it appeared to the Greek mind. A writer of the Aristotelian school plainly says, "It would be ridiculous to accuse God because the love one receives in return from him is not equal to the love given to Him."[5] Christianity changed all this. In Christianity, there is this double movement of God's faith and love going out toward us and of our faith and love in response reaching out to him. The measure of his faith in us, being perfect, involves the terrible responsibility that we should not traduce a love so mighty by acting as cads and becoming reprobate. For this reason the keynote of all our Christian action becomes *loyalty*. It is the characteristic of a fellowship that action within it is directed by loyalty. As Josiah Royce said, *"In loyalty, when loyalty is properly defined, is the fulfilment of the whole moral law."*[6] But if, as we have claimed, God is now revealed in the church, this loyalty must be given to the church, which is the focus of the movement from God to us. Protestants, especially since the nineteenth century, have been slow to acknowledge any kind of authority in the church. Disciples of Christ, in their early history, had a different attitude in this matter; but in the latter part of the nineteenth century, they tended to conform to the general Protestant pattern. A welcome return to their former emphasis is seen in Charles Clayton Morrison's Lyman Beecher Lectures, 1939, *What Is Christianity?*

The question of authority, involving, as it does, the nature of the church as the organ through which Christ acts, is one which has come to divide between Catholics and Protestants in our day. Numbers of clichés are bandied about, such as that Catholics believe in an infallible church and Protestants in an infallible Bible. All such clichés are no more than half-truths. This one, for instance, involves the notion that church and New Testament are in opposition to each other, which is demonstrably false even to the Catholic understanding. There is no possibility of pitting the church against the New Testament, as though one could be superior to the other. What we have to remember is that the gospel, the actual redemptive work of Christ, though it contains the church, is prior both to the empirical church and to the New Testament. The church itself must always be under the judgment of this gospel or word of God, which provides the only standard by which true development can be distinguished from dissolution. But where is this word of God adequately reflected except in the documents of the New Testament, set in the life of the church and historically interpreted? In this sense, the New Testament provides the norm by which all future developments must be tested and therefore holds a unique place. To this unique place both Catholics and Protestants witness. The witness of Protestantism will not be denied. The witness of Catholicism is registered in the place occupied by Epistle and Gospel in the liturgy and in other ways. Nevertheless, Catholics are apt to forget that the church must constantly be brought under the judgment of the word of God.

If we look at Protestantism and Catholicism today in their most absolute forms, we see that the real difference between them is the question of the seat of authority.\* Both agree that ultimately Jesus is the

---

\*The material of the following four and a half pages has been taken almost verbatim from my contribution to *Ministry and Sacraments,* ed., A. C. Headlam. Used by permission of the Student Christian Movement Press.

source of authority in the church. Protestants claim that the authority of Jesus is to be found in the New Testament alone (*sola Scriptura*); though, paradoxically enough, they often emphasize to an extraordinary degree the present-day witness of the Holy Spirit and urge the necessity of moving with the times. The extreme liberal Protestant cry of "Back to Jesus" was so tied up with the desire to be modern in all things that Jesus was conceived of as a conventional twentieth century gentleman![7] On the other hand, Catholics claim that the authority of Jesus is to be found in the church, the church being before the New Testament in time and "the pillar and bulwark of the truth" (1 Tim. 3:15). For them the living body functions as the organ of authority in every age. This doctrine, it would appear, should allow for development (as Newman claimed, over against Protestantism) and should enable the Catholic Church to be the most sensitive of all to the witness of the Holy Spirit in our day. But its implications have often received no more than lip service from Catholics, especially in the West, since the post-Reformation period of intransigence set in. The dangers of this doctrine were clearly revealed in the modernist movement, a generation ago, when theology came near to being reduced, not only to a philosophy of history, but a history without historical foundations.[8] So that Catholics, paradoxically enough, have generally been the more insistent on appealing to what is primitive.

Historical and literary criticism, as well as *Formgeschichte*, have shown that we cannot get back to the historical Jesus beyond the picture of him formed in the mind of the earliest Christian community; though we have been shown at the same time that this is a very reliable picture, and that in the Gospels there is reflected in a most adequate way the mind and spirit of Christ. But we do not see or hear Christ apart from the church; and the whole trouble on the question of authority has come through setting the New Testament over against the church, or the church over against the New Testament. This our early Disciple teachers saw quite clearly. Although they claimed, and rightly claimed, that if we wish to know what Christianity is, we must go to the New Testament documents, and to these documents alone, they had no illusions as to the church's being before the New Testament. And they were definite about two things: first, they were definite in rejecting the Protestant doctrine of *private* interpretation;[9] and second, they were equally definite about the authority of the church. They saw quite clearly that to overstress the authority of the church and to neglect the authority of the New Testament was a movement in the direction of *sub-*

*jectivity* and not of *objectivity*, as might be supposed—
a movement which might quite easily result in reduc-
ing the church to the level of a human society and the
Christian faith to the level of a theosophy wholly
divorced from historicity.[10] The New Testament,
which was a collection of the earliest Christian literature, differed from other Christian literature because
it contained the record of the *creative* Christian experience and witnessed to the life, faith, and spirit of apostolic Christianity. That is why it was to them the
*norm* by which all future developments in the church
must be tested. As such, it was a bulwark against all
subjectivisms and the guarantee of objectivity and
givenness in the Christian system. It had relevance
for the *creative period* of church history, which alone
could have significance for what was the fundamental
and peculiar genius of Christianity.

But they saw with equal clearness that to overstress
the authority of the New Testament, as against that of
the church as an ontological reality with historic continuity, was to make of Christianity a "book religion"
and to reduce the New Testament to the level of the
rulebook, giving rein to private interpretations of a
literalist and legalistic kind.[11] It was this attitude toward the New Testament which had produced the
multiplicity of warring sects, so unlovely in their intransigence, and themselves a contradiction of the

[ 133 ]

*divine* nature of the church. So, while stressing the importance of the New Testament and urging a return to New Testament Christianity, early Disciple teachers declared that no interpretation of the Scriptures was authoritative unless supported by the considered, qualified, scholarship of the church catholic. The great doctors and teachers of the whole church (now unhappily divided) in all ages must be appealed to. This meant that what they sought in the Scriptures was not a *final* and *absolute* interpretation, but an *authoritative* one. They set the Scriptures within the *living* institution and so allowed for development of thought and the spirit of inquiry. They recognized that subtle combination of freedom with loyalty to the church which was characteristic of the church of the early Fathers, but which has largely been lost sight of in the West.

This emphasis on "church *and* New Testament," over against "church *or* New Testament," as well as over against the doctrine of *sola Scriptura*, is surely sound wisdom, for if we put reliance on the New Testament as conveying to us a sure word of God, we must remember that it is the church which gives it its sanction; and if we put reliance on the authority of the church, we must remember that it was the word of God which called it into being and which forever preserves it from becoming a mere human society, providing it with a theology which is not a mere philosophy of religion or a psychology of limited experience and with an ecclesiology which is not a following of human taste or caprice.

How does the church most securely receive the guidance of God and realize her divine character? I would claim that two things are necessary: (*a*) the attitude of worship and (*b*) that she should be under the judgment of the word of God. If the real basis of worship is communion or fellowship—fellowship with God in Christ and with one another—then the church will most fully realize and actualize her divine character in worship. The double movement, from God to us and from us to God, finds its perfect balance in the act of worship, where "infinite passion and the pain of finite hearts that yearn"[12] is fully satisfied. It is in worship that we come fully within "the understanding distance," and in this atmosphere the church can express a "sure word of God." That the church is the instrument through which God acts makes it essential that the *whole* church should express its voice.[13] But that it is God who is acting and not merely man, makes it essential that the whole procedure, whenever the church makes pronouncements or elects to office, should be as far removed from business and political procedure as possible, and that it should have about it the atmosphere of the heavenly plane, for it is only in worship that the heavenly and earthly planes meet, and what is ordinary becomes transmuted into something sublime, what is an event becomes a miracle of grace, and what is historical becomes invested with eternal significance. This is what lies behind the Quaker theory of corporate guidance and the Orthodox theory of worship. It follows that no election is a true election unless it is itself an act of worship and not a business decision; no pronouncement is a true pronouncement if it is the result of a *managed* consensus, rather than of a free consensus.

It is this theory of worship, too, which makes the sermon, when it is delivered as an act of worship, not merely an address or pronouncement of an individual opinion, but the declaration of a true word of God. It also lies behind the distinction between a church theology and private opinion or theologoumena.

Whenever the church corporately yields herself to God, he guides her and acts through her. She becomes so completely one with him that her actions become his actions, possessing the seal of his witness. But this is always provided that her yielding is not the suppression of those qualities of intellect, affection, and conscience which are his gifts to her and which, in the act of worship, become garnished with a due humility, producing a judgment characterized by self-discipline. Apart from the worship attitude, these gifts are bound to minister to self-conceit or spiritual pride, resulting in spiritual blindness and deafness, thus producing a knowledge which is foolishness because it is at bottom a refusal to accept and respond to the love which is at the heart of reality.[14] All such knowledge may be classed as "gnosis falsely so-called"—a refusal to accept the isness of things.[15]

If the church prefers to conduct elections to sacred office and to arrive at her dogmatic pronouncements in the atmosphere of canvassing and lobbying, of gossip and personal preferences and dislikes, doing things "from partiality" (1 Tim. 5:21), she can expect no better results than the methods imply; and she may, in the course of her history, become so lacking in reconciliation to the will of the Father that she becomes a contradiction of his essential character as placarded on the plane of history in revelation. She may refuse to be *his* body and seek *her own* prestige, refusing to bear in her life the marks of her Lord's suffering that she might also share *his* glory.

This brings us to discuss more closely what is the essential character of God which the word of God reveals, under whose judgment the church must ever come, and which the church must reflect in the world. It is the hidden secret which could never have been guessed at. It is the secret that God is redemptive love, and that redemptive love goes *all the way* in suffering, even to the cross; the secret which needed the witness of the actual cross before it could be grasped and believed. It was this secret which our Lord, during his ministry, was struggling to impart to his disciples, those who were to be the foundation stones of the church (Eph. 2:20), and who were to give it the character of apostolicity. The Synoptic Gospels show this quite clearly. In the first period of the ministry—the period of open teaching—the secret is only hinted at and hidden away in parables. Then Jesus chooses the Twelve *to be with him,* and they go away for a period of "teaching by fellowship." At the end of this period comes the Confession at Caesarea Philippi. They had come through to some understanding of his mission, but it was only a partial understanding. Immediately he reveals the hidden secret that the Son of man must go up to Jerusalem and be put to death. But the Twelve, in the person of Peter, reject it. From that time on he begins to teach them *by action*—he sets his face steadfastly toward Jerusalem, and, finally on the cross, divinity is seen at a maximum—the glory of God is completely revealed, for God set him forth (exposed him) to declare both his righteousness and forbearance (long-suffering), to declare that he is not indifferent to sin, and the fact of its costingness to him (Rom. 3:24–26).

The same facts are further illumined by the Fourth Gospel, which is none the less significant because of its foreshortening of time.[16]  A significant chapter is the sixteenth, which comes as the climax of the discourses in the Upper Room.  These discourses all center in the attempt to convey to the disciples the hidden secret about God.  Here, because the perspective is different, the chapter opens with a description of the suffering church and not the suffering Christ (vss. 1-4).  But the suffering Christ and the suffering church are, in the deepest sense, one.  Significantly enough, the chapter closes with the same double reference to the suffering Christ and the suffering church (vss. 32-33).  There are various reasons given why this hidden secret had not been made plain before.  It had not been revealed because Christ was with them (vs. 4), or again, because they were not able to bear it (vs. 12), or because it had been possible to utter it only in parables (vs. 25).  But, in a crisis act, it was to be made plain:  he was going to him that sent him, a reference to his death (vs. 5); he was to glorify the Father (in this Gospel, his death is spoken of as his being glorified); he was to show them plainly of the Father (vs. 25).  In this crisis act (love in action), the nature and character of the Father as redemptive love was to be set forth— the fact that God is the Servant of his servants.[17]

[ 139 ]

It was Plato's firm belief that "no philosophical truth [I should prefer to say "deep truth"] could be communicated in writing at all; it was only by some sort of immediate contact that one soul could kindle the flame in another";[18] and this is what Jesus said in another way when questioned by his disciples as to why he hid away the "secrets of the kingdom of God" in parables. He replied, "To you it has been given to know the secrets of the kingdom of God; but for others they are in parables, so that seeing they may not see, and hearing they may not understand" (Luke 8:10).[19] This is not a "hard saying." It merely states a truth about the nature of things as they are. We can never understand any great teacher until we come within "the understanding distance,"[20] and this can be reached only by great effort and at a great cost to ourselves. Unless we are willing to sacrifice much, there are some deep truths we shall never learn.[21] This is why Jesus placed much emphasis on the *moral* attitude in learning. There is about all truth which is worth while a certain incommunicable character. It can be "caught" only by those who are *en rapport* with the teacher. All such truth is destroyed by codification and legal structure. It can be preserved only in societies of choice souls through a visible fellowship. The truth which is in Jesus Christ needs for its full understanding and application to life such a society living together in a love relationship. Thus it comes about that the church in history becomes the sure witness to the fact that *fellowship* is the hidden structure of reality. . Hence the intense prayer that the church might be one, that the world might believe the apostolical character of the Christ—that he was in actuality the penetration of the eternal into history, the true portrayal of the character of the Father (John, chap. 17). The apostolicity of the church is to be recognized in the same way: "By this shall all men know that you are my disciples, if you have love for one another" (John 13:35). By her actualizing of such fellowship, she not only declares the truth that "happiness consisteth not of lordship over one's neighbour, nor in desiring to have more than weaker men, nor in possessing wealth and using force to inferiors," and makes undeniable the fact that "God's greatness is not of this order" (*Epistle to Diognetus*, VII); but she herself becomes the "salt of the earth" and makes history meaningful and purposeful.

There is always, however, the dreadful prospect that the salt "may lose its savor." This is surely what happens whenever the church ceases to be a true *servus servorum*. The real sin of the church is imperialism —savoring of man and not of God—what the Gospels refer to as "the way of the Gentiles." When the church forsakes the way of service and seeks power,

[ 141 ]

*Like Shark*

she denies her own nature and the character of the God whom she seeks to worship (see Matt. 18:1-4; 6:32; Mark 10:42; Luke 22:25). This means that we ought to distinguish clearly between two kinds of schism in the history of the church. First there is the schism which divides within the church and which may be called "dogmatic schism"; and second, the schism which divides between the church and the state, which may be called "political schism." This second kind of schism occurs when the "great church" becomes Erastian in temper and compromises with the world, is filled with worldly ambition, and seeks power instead of love. Then, as has happened, a group may break away in rebellion against such a betrayal of her true character; and such a group may, in a sense, be regarded as the true church, as over against the "great church." There can be no doubt that from the time of Constantine, this was the church's greatest temptation. There can be little doubt that in theMiddle Ages, through force of circumstances, the church fell deeply into this sin, but never so far as to lose completely the marks of apostolicity. The error of the modern Roman Church is not so much in her catholicism as in her imperialism. In the case of "dogmatic schism," it would have been well if only those heresies had been allowed as real heresies where the rejected dogma in question embodied within itself a contradiction of the essential nature of the church as the true *servus servorum*, as was the case with Docetism. The church has had far too little faith that truth would prevail.

It is when the church, humbling herself before her Lord, retains her Christlike (Godlike) character, which in a world such as this is set forth as redemptive suffering, that she is seen as divine and that she can be sure of the guidance of God. This is her true apostolical character, and it is the denial of this apostolical character which has been her chief sin through the ages.

# VII

## THE CHURCH IN HISTORY

WE COME now to the difficult question of how the church perpetuates herself in history. How does she remain the *same* church and yet not the same? We may reject at once the notion that the church can *start afresh* in any age—that she is merely a *free association* of men and women who pledge themselves by a certain loyalty to Christ and to one another, a theory which bears a striking resemblance to Hobbes's theory of the state and which, indeed, had its rise in the same set of circumstances. If the church is the fulfillment in time of the activity of the Word of God which began with the first creative act, she must have historic continuity of some kind.

Neither is it merely the *function* of the church and not the *form* that must live on. With the church it must be true, to quote Wordsworth's famous line, that "the Form remains, the Function never dies." We may, likewise, reject those theories of the church which regard its continuity as being maintained wholly within the *invisible* sphere, and which speak of the invisible church as the true church, as over against the historic church.[1] Spiritual continuity alone is not compatible with the Christian revelation of the word of

[ 145 ]

God. It would be compatible with a system which built itself up on a one-way movement, either from God to us (transcendence), or from us to God (immanence); but it is quite incompatible with a system which is neither deistic nor pantheistic, but is built up on the paradox of transcendence with immanence. Such a system, as we have seen, is demanded by the Christian revelation, which sees this transcendent-immanent relationship of God to the cosmos coming to a focus in the "Word made flesh" and reaching a limit of concretion in a living personality.[2] As with Christ, so with the church there must be the expression of the inner function by an outer form.

But neither must we think of the continuity of the church as being maintained wholly within the *form* or structure of the church, for such is not the way that historic continuity is preserved in a *living* reality. To maintain it in the case of the Christian church would be to deny the heart of the Christian revelation, which is that God is in *personal* and not mechanical or legal relationship to his people, and that the church is the *fellowship*. We shall have to put out of our minds any conceptions of continuity which have a mechanical or legalistic form.

In the present situation of a divided church, we may find some relief in Troeltsch's distinction between "catholic" and "sect" types of Christianity and maintain that both are necessary to the continuity of the church, each living and maintaining itself in opposition to the other, and yet each contributing vitality and existence to the other in this very opposition. Indeed, we may see some analogy to this in the "spiritual Israel" within the "great Israel," and we may even note that the members of the "spiritual Israel" were often outside the hierarchy proper, and that our Lord himself had a priesthood which was after the pattern of Melchizedek and not after the pattern of Aaron—a priesthood without beginning or end. We may go even further, as Troeltsch does, and see the necessity for such duality grounded within the nature of reality itself in its temporal and concrete form. But this means two things. It means that the "sect" type must abandon alike the theory that the church can ever start afresh as the free association of men and women, and the theory that continuity is maintained alone within the function of the church apart from the form, and frankly recognize the necessity of the "catholic" type to her own existence. Secondly, it means that the "catholic" type must abandon the rigid theory (often almost mechanical in form) that the continuity of the church is contained solely within the outward structure, and that validity is to be equated with "order." The "catholic" type must likewise recognize the necessity of the "sect" type for her own vitality, however much she may deplore the lack of form which she discovers in the "sect" type.

If we fall back on Paul's description of the church as the body of Christ, remembering that while for him the expression meant a mystical reality, yet at the same time it carried with it the idea that there was a fundamental analogy between the church and the living physical body, what we have said will gain in sharpness by following up this analogy. The question arises, Does the skeleton or framework form the living body, or does the living body mold and shape the skeleton? The "catholic" type tends to put nearly all the emphasis on the skeleton, as though the skeleton were first shaped and molded and then the body placed upon it.[3] The skeleton, in such a view, often becomes a rigid pattern incapable of growth or development, and the body of little or no importance. The "sect" type, on the other hand, places all the emphasis on the body, as though the body had no form or pattern into which to grow up and was the creator of its own form. In doing this it forgets that while it is possible to have a skeleton without a body (though it would be a pretty dead affair), it is not at all possible to have a body without a skeleton, certainly not a living body which can function. The truth is, of course, that neither does the skeleton form the body, nor the body form the skeleton. Both things happen in a *living* body. There is interaction always going on. This means that the "catholic" type must be prepared to allow for such changes and modifications in the structural form of the church as are compatible with growth, as over against dissolution, and that the "sect" type must be prepared to admit a sufficient measure of structure to guarantee the permanence of the body itself. The first must recognize the truth of the proverb, *Cela change le moins qui change le plus,* and the other must recognize the truth of the proverb, *Cela change le plus qui change le moins.* Both can be true only within a *living* concrete reality. But when this double recognition is effected, the "catholic" and "sect" types will no longer be organically separated from each other. The "great church" will bear within herself the double witness,[4] for there must always be in a *living* reality this tension of seeming opposites.

If, then, we accept the fact that the continuity of the church must be maintained within its structure, as well as within its function, we have now to inquire what this structural continuity must consist of in order that the apostolicity of the church may be guaranteed. The church, as we have seen, is essentially living. Yet while life is not organization, it remains true that no life can express itself unless it is organized. But the structure must be compatible with the livingness of the body, with the function which it articulates.

Historically speaking, it cannot be denied that the church was first organized around the apostolic ministry. That ministry was the organ through which the church expressed her authority. However the accounts vary, it seems clear that the apostles received their commission from the living Lord (Matt. 10:5, 16; 16:19; 18:18; Mark 3:14; Luke 10:3; John 17:18; 20:21-23). But were the apostles one thing and the church another, or were the apostles the church in embryo? Did the apostles come first, and was the church added to them, as seems to be suggested in *The Apostolic Ministry* at some points?[5] This view, which is often suggested by Catholic writers, seems to me to ignore the intimate relationship between the Head and the church and between the "foundation stones" and the church. If we are to think of the church *organically*, and if we remember that there is also a real connection between the "old Israel" and the "new Israel," it would appear that any separation of the apostles from the church is too *static* a view to cover the real facts. Neither can we ignore the fact that at Pentecost, according to the most probable interpretation of the second chapter of Acts, the Holy Spirit was given to *the church as such*, which included "the Twelve." Further, whatever authority the apostles have, they do not exercise it from *without*

the church, but from *within*. They also are members
of the church. To set the hierarchy and the church
apart, as though the hierarchy were one thing and the
church another, is to misunderstand the nature of the
church.

Such thinking would have been impossible in the
first five centuries of church history. In the Middle
Ages such thinking becomes predominant. Salvation
and damnation become the sole prerogatives of the
clergy, with the sacrament of penance as the major
sacrament. Private Masses are another example of
the same tendency. It is this medieval influence which
has lived on to our day, and in other churches than
those which are traditionally Catholic, which is aptly
described by Daniel Jenkins in these words:

> The ordinary member has little opportunity of expressing
> his membership of the Church except through attendance at
> Divine Service and his obedience to his pastors. Indeed, he
> is not so much a member of the Church, through whom the
> life-blood of the Church flows, as a person who derives his
> spiritual sustenance from the Church, which appears to exist
> in some way independently of him.

> The congregation are the "dear children" of the hier-
> archy. But in point of fact they are nothing of the kind.
> They are the brethren of their ministers and have a right to
> protest when it is assumed that they should be fed on milk,
> as babes in Christ, and that the meat should be reserved for
> the "religious."[6]

This raises the important question as to whether the commission is given to the apostles as such, or whether it is given to the church as represented by the apostles. I should suggest that the answer is in neither of these alternatives, but in both. The authority which the apostles have is from Christ, but it is not authority *over* the church, but authority *in* the church. Authority in the church, even apostolic authority, is unlike authority in any other corporation. The church is neither a democracy nor an autocracy, and authority is never judicial. The church is a family, and those who have pastoral authority in the church exercise it in the manner of oversight (*episcopē*), and this is as true of the original apostles as of those to whom authority was delegated by them. Pastors act as "fathers in God" to the family, and this is a proper way of looking at the matter, providing we recognize that the word "children" refers, not only to children in the ordinary sense, but to adult children.

It is equally clear that authority within the church (of the kind we have indicated) was delegated by the rite of ordination, and thus the apostolic ministry was handed on from age to age within the church. The evidence, both from the New Testament and the Apostolic Fathers, it seems to me, is so clear that it is hardly worth discussing. The idea suggested by

Canon Streeter that everything in this area was loose and subject to opportunism is both whimsical and fantastic. But does this involve the acceptance of the rigid theory of apostolic succession as it is held by Western Catholics, carrying with it the idea that validity, rather than regularity, is bound up with such a succession? It is generally assumed by those who take this position that apostolic succession is necessary to a sacramental view of ordination, but it would be easy to show from information coming to us from the first and second centuries that such an assumption is without support, especially if we mean by succession a succession of bishops.[7] For a *mechanical* view it is necessary, but not for a sacramental view.

The theory of apostolic succession starts with the idea that the commission of our Lord was given to the apostles as such, and not to the church, and goes on to claim that the bishops, as an order, are the natural successors of the apostles and do not derive from the body of presbyters.[8] Sometimes, when it is held, this theory goes to the length of making the ministry vicarious and sacerdotal; but, on the other hand, such a champion of the theory as Dr. Gore was definite that the ministry was representative. All early evidence is on the side of the minister's being regarded as representative, though he was not merely representative of the congregation. He was also the minister of

Christ. But *how* was he the minister of Christ? Was it through a definite channel of apostolic succession that this power of making men Christ's ministers flowed? Or was the power vested in the church as the body of Christ? Was it due to the fact that when the church gave herself up to the guidance of God through his Spirit, there was a true choice and a true ordination by Christ? Is not the latter view more in keeping with the "high" doctrine of the church that she is the body of Christ, in personal, living relationship with her Head, ministers being the organs of the body, through whom she functions? And is not the former more in keeping with "high clericalism" than with a "high" doctrine of the church?

The doctrine of apostolic succession claims that the apostles and apostolic-men were the only ones who ordained anybody in the first age; and, on historical grounds, this is difficult to support.[9] In any case, if apostolic succession was essential, it is difficult to account for Paul's negligence in such churches as Corinth and Rome, where it is clear that the single bishop arose late. We do know that in going to Rome he desired to impart some spiritual gift to the church, but we know nothing of his desiring to impart the power of ordination to an individual. The argument for a second Apostolic Council, advanced by Rothe, can hardly carry much weight after its refutation by Lightfoot[10] and others. The first real passage advanced in favor of apostolic succession is that of Clement of Rome (A.D. 96), but it is clear, as Lightfoot has shown, that it cannot bear the interpretation put upon it as the only valid exegesis. Gregory Dix seems to be conscious of this, and though he himself accepts the exegesis which gives effect to the doctrine of apostolic succession, he is fully aware of the fact that there are strong grounds for a different interpretation.[11] In any case, Clement knows nothing of bishops, in the later sense of the term, so whatever his view of transmission, it supports transmission through presbyters (though they may be presbyters possessing *episcopē*), as much as transmission through bishops. Neither Ignatius nor Polycarp says anything about the doctrine of apostolic succession, and it is difficult to imagine that Ignatius would neglect to produce it in support of his teaching on submission to the bishop with his presbyters. If anyone stands in the place of the apostles in Ignatius' opinion, it appears to be the presbyters rather than the bishop.[12]

The first to mention unequivocally a succession of bishops is Irenaeus. But apart from some difficulties in connection with the text of the passage, we should carefully note what Irenaeus is really doing.[13] He is contending with Gnostics who claim that they have received by transmission some *secret* teaching not known in catholic churches. Irenaeus has two arguments against this: (*a*) there can be only four Gospels, and the teaching in question must be in these, or in the tradition which has come down in a regular manner; (*b*) this tradition, if it is found anywhere, will be found in the great churches established by the apostles, and in these it is possible to trace the bishops back to the apostles. It is ridiculous, for instance, for Gnostics to claim that they have some secret treasure of knowledge, in view of the fact that Paul was in Rome and knew Linus. To whom would Paul have delivered it if not to Linus? And to whom would Linus have delivered it if not to Anicletus? And so on. It should be noted that Irenaeus does not state that Linus *succeeded* the apostles, but received from them the office of bishop or oversight. It is not of any handing on of the power of ordination that he speaks, but of the handing on of true doctrine. As late as the fifth century, Jerome, who is content to allow that only bishops should ordain, still knows nothing of apostolic succession in its rigid doctrinal form.

It is easy to see how, after the dying out of the apostles and evangelists (who appear to have been apostolic-men), bishops would naturally be sought for ordinations, especially those who themselves had been appointed by apostolic-men. The desire for unity at the turn of the century and in the second century, which was coupled with the battle against Docetism, and later with the battle against a full-blown Gnosticism, would strengthen this trend, and lists of bishops, as heads of the churches, would serve a useful purpose against Gnostic claims. (Lists of presbyters would have been somewhat more difficult to prepare.) But this slender foundation simply will not bear the structure of the doctrine of apostolic succession which has been reared upon it.

While it may be admitted that from the end of the second century down to the Reformation, the structure of the church was bound up with the episcopal form, and that from a somewhat later date this structure was bound up with the idea of ordination transmitted through a succession of bishops, and while we may allow on this account a peculiar measure of authority to attach to such a structure, it is a very different thing when we invest this structure with validity, rather than regard it as providing a guarantee of regularity. Apart from the fact that such a theory of validity would need to build a stronger bridge over the first two centuries than it is able to do with the available facts, or indeed than it is legitimate to do in the face of some facts which are available, we have to remember that just as strong a case can be made out in the first two centuries for presbyterial succession as for episcopal succession. And, further, we have to remember that since the Reformation, in those churches which broke away from Rome and retained the episcopal ministry, the rigid theory of apostolic succession was not at first carried over with the episcopal ministry, and ministers ordained by presbyterial ordination were accepted by them as true ministers of the word and of the sacraments. In the case of the Swedish and Finnish churches, they have always continued to recognize the validity of orders other than those conferred by episcopal ordination. In the case of the Anglican Church, the attitude on this question has varied within the church itself, whatever the Ordinal prescribes, and still does vary today. In the sixteenth century, Presbyterian orders were accepted as valid by the Anglican Church, and Bucer and Peter Martyr were actually made professors of theology at Oxford and Cambridge. Till the middle of the seventeenth century, it would appear that there was no real ground of quarrel between the Anglican and Continental churches on the question of orders. Hooker, as the chief Anglican authority, as over against the Puritans, declares that "there may be sometimes very just and sufficient reason to allow

ordination made without a Bishop.''[14] The matter is
further dealt with by Richard Field in his work, *Of
the Church*, published in 1606:

> For if the power of order and authority to intermeddle in
> things pertaining to God's service be the same in all presby-
> ters, and that they be limited in the execution of it only for
> Order's sake, so that in the case of necessity everyone of them
> may baptize, and confirm them whom they have baptized,
> absolve and reconcile penitents, and do all those other acts
> which regularly are appropriated unto the bishop alone; there
> is no reason to be given, but that in the case of necessity,
> wherein all bishops were extinguished by death, or being
> fallen into heresy, should refuse to ordain any to serve God
> in His true worship, but that presbyters, as they may do all
> other acts, whatsoever special challenge bishops in ordinary
> course make upon them, might do this also. Who then dare
> condemn all those worthy ministers of God that were or-
> dained by presbyters in sundry Churches of the world, at
> such times as bishops, in those parts where they lived, opposed
> themselves against the truth of God and persecuted such as
> professed it? Surely the best learned in the Church of Rome
> in former times durst not pronounce all ordinations of this
> nature to be void. For not only Armachanus (*Lib.* X, 9,
> *Armenorum, cap.* 7), a very learned and worthy bishop, but
> as it appeareth by Alexander of Hales, many learned men in
> his time and before were of the opinion that in some cases,
> and in some times presbyters may give Orders, and that
> their ordinations are of force, though to do so—not being
> urged by extreme necessity—cannot be excused from over
> great boldness and presumption. Neither should it seem so

strange to our adversaries [Roman Catholics], that the power of ordination should at some times be yielded unto presbyters, seeing that *chorepiscopi*, suffragans, and titular bishops, and are no bishops, according to the old course of discipline, do daily in the Romish Church, both confirm children and give Orders.[15]

The famous case of the ordination of the three Scottish bishops in 1610 put the whole matter to the test. The question arose as to whether these three men were first to be ordained deacons and then priests before being consecrated bishops. The whole matter was discussed before the Archbishop of Canterbury (Bancroft), who agreed that there was no necessity to follow this course, "seeing where Bishops could not be had, the ordination given by the Presbyters must be esteemed lawful."[16] This explanation of the act must be accepted, or otherwise we must conclude with Heylyn that the action was justified on the ground of ordination *per saltum;* and this is a most precarious position to take for those who wish to defend the rigid theory of apostolic succession through bishops, for while it is true that ordinations to the episcopate *per saltum* were normal in the primitive age, they were so because the later conception of orders was unknown. Moreover, all Roman canonists are agreed that such ordination is irregular and without validity.[17]

Enough has been said, and much more could be said, on this point to show that *validity* cannot be equated with *regularity* nor made to depend on it too rigidly. In the rigid theory of apostolic succession which develops from the fifth century onward in the form of a succession of orders, or, more strictly speaking, of ordainers, the church comes to be almost completely left out of account altogether. In the ordination of titular bishops, it has altogether disappeared. In the primitive church of the first five centuries, if the various grades of the hierarchy have a liturgy, so has the laity a liturgy; and without both, the liturgy itself is incomplete. One thing the Reformation did was to attempt to recover this conception and to bring the church, God's faithful people, back into the picture. It did not altogether succeed, because the Reformers themselves were blinded by certain medieval preconceptions. In the separatist movement in England, it succeeded better, for the early Congregationalists and Baptists did recover the idea of the "gathered community," each with its pastor and other shepherds of the flock.[18] Another thing the Reformation did do was to deny that the "living community" could be bound too closely to a set form. No doubt Protestant churches have sprung too far to the other side in denying the necessity of "order" of any kind, but the essential truth that spiritual values cannot be tied irrevocably to set forms—this they will not give up. In this matter I find myself in agreement with William Temple, the late Archbishop of Canterbury, when he says:*

> Now if it be held that episcopal ordination confers a *power* of making sacraments, so that when an episcopally ordained priest celebrates the Eucharist something happens in the world of fact which does not happen on any other condition, then these bodies [nonepiscopal churches] have no real Sacraments. But that is a theory to which I find myself unable to attach any intelligible meaning. It is admitted that the peril to which strong sacramental doctrine is most liable is that of falling into conceptions properly described as magical; and this theory seems to me to lie on the wrong side of the dividing line. What is conferred in Ordination is not the *power* to make sacramental a rite which otherwise would not be such, but *authority* (*potestas*) to administer Sacraments which belong to the Church, and which, therefore, can only be rightly administered by those who hold the Church's commission to do so. The objection to lay celebration is not that it is in its own nature inoperative, but that it is a usurpation by one member of what belongs to the whole Church. Strictly speaking, I submit, we should not say that a layman cannot celebrate, but that he has no right to celebrate, and it would therefore be wrong for him to do so.

> But, it will be urged, we are not concerned with lay-celebration, but with ministries accredited in their own parts of the Church. That is for the most part true; but the first

*Thoughts on Some Problems of the Day*, pp. 110-11. Used by permission of the Macmillan Co., London.

point on which it is necessary to be clear is whether we regard
the action of the Church in Ordination as so related to the
Sacraments that where there is no episcopally ordained priest
there is no real Sacrament. I find that position untenable,
and even in the last resort unintelligible.

I submit that such a position is more in keeping with
the true nature of the church as *personally* and not mechanically or legally related to God. The apostolic
character of the church depends on the apostolic commission given by our Lord to his apostles and transmitted by them to successive generations of Christian
ministers. This commission is "the mystery of godli-
ness," "the saving word of God," which is contained
in word and sacrament. The intention of our Lord
was doubtless the intention of the apostles when they
commissioned the first apostolic delegates, and again
of those who succeeded them, as it has been, and is, of
all the great representative churches. Where such intention is clear, we cannot raise questions of validity,
nor raise doubts as to apostolic character, though we
may have to discuss questions of regularity, if we are
to fashion a structure for the church which will at once
guarantee her continuity with the church in all ages,
and provide a true vehicle for the expression of her
life as she actually is and must be in this age. But in
all we do, we shall have to remember that in a church
which is not only the guardian of the word of God, but

which is the vehicle through which the *living* Word of God is manifested in the time process, apostolicity can never be mainly concerned with questions of mechanical or legal descent. In such a church we shall have to allow for creativity; for "the word of God is not fettered" (2 Tim. 2:9).

# VIII

## THE APOSTOLICITY OF THE CHURCH

In THIS chapter it will be necessary to enter more deeply into the controversial issue which is raised between Catholic and Protestant churches as to the question of apostolic succession. Does the apostolicity of the church consist in the fact that the true church exists wherever the word of God is preached and the sacraments administered according to the word of God, as all the great Protestant Confessions declare; or does it also require that there should be in the church a duly appointed apostolic ministry in direct succession from the apostles? Not only so, but the issue goes deeper, for it is further claimed that where there is no such ministry, there are no valid sacraments, or at least that there is no valid Eucharist. Let us be quite clear what this means. It does not mean that a Eucharist administered by a minister outside the apostolic succession is necessarily *ineffective* spiritually; but it does mean that it cannot, and does not, carry with it the guarantee that the promise attached to it is realized, because it is not performed by one who has the right to administer it. Neither is it just a matter of maintaining succession with the apostolic church. There are high-church Presbyterians who would maintain that their presbyterial orders are in succession from the apostolic ministry by descent of ordination. For those who rigidly adhere to the doctrine of apostolic succession, this is of no avail, for the only valid ministry is that which has its ordination through a succession of bishops. The right to ordain is not committed to presbyters as such. It was committed by the apostles and by apostolic-men to bishops and to none other. Outside this succession there is no valid ministry and no valid Eucharist.[1]

This is the situation, and it is a serious one. On one side of the cleavage stand the Roman Church, the Eastern Orthodox Church, the Old Catholic Church, and some Anglo-Catholics.[2] On the other side stand the major Protestant churches, some of which, like the Church of Sweden, have the episcopal succession, regarding it as of the *bene esse* of the church rather than as of the *esse* of the church. There are many within the Anglican (Protestant Episcopal) Church who also hold to the position that episcopacy is of the *bene esse* of the church, and not of the *esse* of the church; but any move on their part toward the full and complete recognition of nonepiscopal ministries would split the Anglican Church from top to bottom. The union scheme which in South India has been consummated between the Episcopal Church in South India, the

South India United Church (Presbyterians and Congregationalists), and the Methodist Church in South India, is based upon the compromise of an interim period, in which all ministries now in existence in the uniting churches will be recognized, but in future all ministers will be episcopally ordained.[3] It is often claimed that episcopacy can be accepted without the theory of apostolic succession connected with it. But can it? Episcopacy as a form of church polity and nothing more, could be. But this would not involve placing a particular ministry within the apostolic succession. It is precisely this entering the line of succession which is being demanded. The succession was broken in the sixteenth century and must be restored. This is the demand which is made in all cases of regularizing a particular ministry. It is futile to attempt to evade the issue. It must be squarely faced. Does episcopal succession, in the sense that it is essential to a valid ministry and hence to a valid Eucharist, belong to the apostolicity of the church, to the essential structure of the church?

I have already admitted that on the Protestant side, there is often a serious lack of concern about questions of structure, even an impatience with such questions. This lack of concern is a definite weakness in Protestantism, and the impatience is a real hindrance to any fruitful understanding between Protestants and

Catholics on the matter. Karl Barth has said, "There is one fundamental ecclesiastical principle which cannot be denied without at the same time denying the resurrection of Christ and in so doing the very heart of the entire New Testament: the authority of the Apostolate."[4] So often Protestants speak as though there were no essential structure in the New Testament church. This is a serious weakness, and it causes Catholics of all shades, many of whom probably overemphasize structure and introduce into it elements which have no proper place, to be suspicious. At least the Catholic, in his emphasis on structure, is concerned for the unity of the church, while the Protestant, with his unconcern about matters of structure, seems to him to have no more than a sentimental interest in unity. Protestantism does need to recover the sense of the apostolicity of the church and of the reality of the apostolic authority in the primitive church.

Believing this most sincerely, I want to examine the claim for apostolicity through episcopal succession, which is put forward from the Anglo-Catholic side. I do so in no polemical spirit, but as of necessity, and in a spirit which I hope may be irenic. There have recently appeared in the Anglican Church three books of importance on this question, and to these I shall mostly refer. The first is *The Way of At-one-ment*, by Canon W. J. Phythian-Adams, of Carlisle Cathedral, an Anglo-Catholic and an original Old Testament scholar, who until recently was editor of the *Church Quarterly Review*. The second is *The Form of the Church*, by Father A. G. Hebert, of the Society of the Sacred Mission, Kelham, who is an advocate of biblical theology within the Anglo-Catholic fold. The third is the massive work on *The Apostolic Ministry*, edited by Dr. Kenneth E. Kirk, the present Bishop of Oxford, and contributed to by a group of Anglo-Catholic scholars, both men and women, including Father Hebert, but not Canon Phythian-Adams. The chief of these scholars is Dom Gregory Dix, monk of Nashdom Abbey, who is among the foremost liturgiologists of our day. His essay on "The Ministry in the Early Church" is among the most able in the book, and certainly is the most revolutionary. Dr. Kirk, the Bishop of Oxford, represents the most rigid and uncompromising form of Anglo-Catholicism in the Church of England today. Between the first of these books and the last, there is a wide gulf, as we shall see, for Canon Phythian-Adams, while he is no less convincedly Catholic in his churchmanship, belongs to a mediating school.

It will be most convenient to start from the eighth chapter of Father Hebert's book, *The Form of the Church*, where he discusses the apostolicity of the church. Few would be found to disagree with him

[ 169 ]

when he begins by claiming that the word "apostolic" primarily belongs to our Lord (see Heb. 3:1). He is the "sent One," sent from the Father. Nor need we quarrel with the tremendous emphasis which, in *The Apostolic Ministry,* is put on the Aramaic word *shaliach,* though we may think it a little unnecessary to drag it in so frequently to emphasize what is so obvious. It is clear that our Lord bears, in his incarnate life, the full authority of the Father who sends him, just as the *shaliach* did, whether he were son or slave. Father Hebert then goes on to describe the redemptive mission of our Lord on which he is sent. He then says, "The Church is apostolic, as entrusted with this same mission."[5] This is a welcome truth which has always been claimed on the Protestant side. This is the first mark of the apostolicity of the church, that she should bear in her own witness, both by proclamation and *by life,* the redemptive message of the gospel of Christ. Further, Protestants will find themselves in hearty agreement with Father Hebert when he says: "The New Testament is the canon, or norm, or standard, by which the teaching given in the Church is to be judged, and to which it must appeal. It is true that the tradition of the Church was in existence before the books of the New Testament were written; but the tradition was at that time in the hands of the Apostles themselves, and the books were written to preserve the tradition as the Apostles gave it."[6] This is the claim made at the Reformation that the church must always be under the judgment of the word of God. That church is apostolic which preserves the apostolic tradition. Some difficulty will be felt, however, when he says that "the Apostles are in an important sense prior to the Church";[7] and again, "The Ministry is the bearer of the mission itself, consisting of the persons made formally responsible for carrying it on, the Apostles and their successors."[8] These two statements are full of large generalization which needs careful and critical examination. The need for this critical examination is seen in that Father Hebert immediately follows the latter passage by plunging into the doctrine of apostolic succession through a succession of consecrators: "The Church is Apostolic in two senses, corresponding to the two meanings of the term 'Apostolic Succession': namely, the succession of bishops in a see, each following his predecessor, and the succession of consecration whereby the ministerial office itself is handed on."[9]

In the first place, are the apostles really *prior to* the church in any sense which would warrant his claim that "the Ministry is the bearer of the mission itself"? This is the crux of the issue at its very source. I have already discussed this question in the previous chapter (pp. 150ff.), where I suggested that the claim is an oversimplification of the matter. The close identity of our Lord himself, the Head of the church, with the church, in his Messianic mission, surely forbids us to separate between the apostles and the church in such a drastic fashion. There is a sense, of course, in which we can think of the church as beginning on the Day of Pentecost, but it is quite inadequate to the dynamic biblical conception of the church. As we have seen, our Lord does not so much *found* the church as *re-create* it, and in re-creating the church, it is not a question of his setting up an institution apart from himself; he brings the church with him. The church is *in* him, and, in one sense, he is the church, the Israel of God. Those whom he calls to be with him in his lifetime are surely also part of the church. If we hold this view, which is more consistent with the biblical doctrine of the church, it is difficult to set the apostles over against the church, whatever measure of authority we may allow them.

The next leap which Father Hebert makes in asserting that the apostolicity of the church consists of apostolic succession in two senses—the succession of the apostolic tradition and the succession of consecrators —is a big one indeed and needs closer examination. With regard to apostolic succession by a succession of consecrators, which is the only real ground of opposition between those who claim apostolic succession as necessary to a valid ministry and those who do not, Gregory Dix, in *The Apostolic Ministry* (p. 201), admits that there is no evidence for it before about A.D. 170, except in the single passage in 1 Clement, which is of doubtful interpretation (see p. 155). When first the idea of succession appears (in the second century), the emphasis is on the official succession of the bishop's dead predecessor in the church, and not on a succession of episcopal consecrators. The idea of a succession of episcopal consecrators, as Gregory Dix admits, finally took root in the church between about 175 and 200. Before that, the emphasis was, as I have said, on the official succession of one bishop to another in each church; and, as Gregory Dix says, "There is in this way of reckoning the matter no emphasis whatever on the *sacramental* 'succession' of a bishop to those bishops of other Churches who had consecrated him to the episcopate by the laying on of hands."[10]  Father Hebert admits: "Episcopacy was not instituted as such by our Lord."[11]  Again, he admits, in his rather loose language, that "we cannot claim that the Three-fold Ministry is of Divine institution, but only that it was found necessary from early times for the Bishop to delegate to the presbyterate all that ministry of the word and sacraments which is necessary for the oversight of a congregation, while he had his deacons as his own assistants."[12]

These are serious admissions. Canon Phythian-Adams is even more downright, for he says: "It is useless, for example, to talk about Apostolic Succession if it simply means an unbroken series of particular manual acts. No thinking man believes that the grace of a personal God is transmitted mechanically."[13] And again, "As I have before argued, it does not matter *who* preaches us the pure Word of God, provided that he has learned what it is: it does not matter *who* gives us the Sacraments, provided he represents the principle of that which he administers."[14] On the question of validity and the administration of the sacraments as being connected with episcopal succession, he is even stronger:

> "Validity" is thus in the last analysis a matter of right intention; the intention to use the sacraments for the purpose for which they were given, i.e., At-one-ment. Just as the man who harbours hate in his heart is "void of prayer and of the Eucharist,"[15] though he receives, so, too, are they whose Eucharist, by whomsoever ministered, is not the consentient offering of the Church. It is not, let it be repeated, that the Bishop possesses a power of consecration which the other celebrant lacks. So far was this from being true in the early Church that in certain circumstances (e.g. of isolation) any Christian could "offer the gift." He acted then in virtue of his participation in the Royal Priesthood and on the principle *"ubi tres, ecclesia est, licet laici"*;[16] and his offering, being that of a consentient body, was perfectly "valid."[17]

[ 174 ]

Phythian-Adams is, of course, aware of all that
has been said about this famous passage from Tertullian, that it belongs to his Montanist period. He
argues that Tertullian could not have used it in the
connection in which he does unless it had been accepted
generally in his day. This, it seems to me, is true
enough, for he is arguing about lay digamy. As the
bishop must be the husband of one wife, so must the
layman, for *in extremis* he has the power both to "offer
the gifts" (to celebrate the Eucharist) and to baptize,
both of which were at that time the functions of the
single bishop in the single church.[18] This does not
mean that Canon Phythian-Adams is insensitive to
the value of episcopacy as the means of preserving the
unity of the church. On the contrary, he stresses its
value, though he recognizes that from age to age the
form of episcopacy has changed and may still change:*

> They [the Anglicans] maintain that episcopal, i.e., hier-
> archical government has come down to us by direct trans-
> mission from the Apostles: and with all respect to our Pres-
> byterian brethren, I am bound to say that all the known facts
> warrant this conclusion. On any other view we should have
> to assume a drastic revolution in Church government, of
> which not the faintest echo has come down to us. But if
> these are the facts, let us remember that they are no more
> than—facts! They tell us how the basic principle of the

*The material that follows is from *The Way of At-one-ment*,
pp. 117-19. Used by permission of the Student Christian Movement Press.

new Life was actually worked out in the Ministry of the Early Church; but it does not follow that the particular series of steps then taken has for all time the force of prescriptive statute. [This] would be sheer antiquarianism. History is contingent, relative: and the only result of thus deifying the acts of our forefathers is to petrify our own. What we have to do is to analyse the established facts in the light of their governing principle, seeking to discover which of them seems essential to its embodiment, and which to be mere expedients of their time. Thus in the former class we shall certainly place the adoption of the Hierarchy, or rather its acceptance from Christ; but we shall also note as an important fact about it that its constituents varied with the condition of the Church's life and growth. On the other hand, it is not easy to discern any essential relevance in the historical development of Episcopacy, for this had its origin *not in any theological principle* [italics mine] but in the pressure of circumstance. The primary unit of fellowship was then found naturally and conveniently within the compass of a small city or market town, and at first it was no larger than what we now call a Congregation: one man, that is to say, could have personal oversight of all its members, whilst its economic needs could be supplied by no more than two deacons. *In spite of this the Pastor charged with the care of so small a flock was a Bishop, invested with full Apostolic authority.* I underline this because it is this, not what subsequently happened, which needs to be remembered. What *happened*, was that as more and more people became Christians the Bishop subdivided his cure among his Presbyters, delegating to each of them a large part of Apostolic authority.[19] But was this a necessary *theological* development? On the face of it certainly not.

[ 176 ]

. . . These considerations suggest that those who advocate Episcopacy must distinguish frankly between two lines of argument. First, there is *theological argument*. This holds that according to the Scriptures the At-one-ment of the Body is built up from the Head through a Hierarchy or descending series of sacred ministers. It maintains further that the Hierarchy is a necessity of the new Life because it is basically inherent in the old: it is the consecration by God of that diversity of special gifts which has already brought man far on the path of common achievement. While, therefore, the Christian Hierarchy may vary in constitution with the needs of the Church, it cannot be dispensed with if the Church is to attain the fulness of its stature in Christ: and in so far as Episcopacy embodies this principle, it should be universally recognized. On the other hand, no claim can be made on theological grounds that all the details of its historical development must be regarded as sacrosanct.

Father Hebert examines six objections offered by nonepiscopal churches to regarding the episcopate as the guardian of the apostolic commission in the church. First is the objection that the apostles, as living witnesses of the Resurrection of our Lord, could have no successors, and therefore all subsequent forms of ministry are purely human expedients. It ought to be said at once that those who hold the first part of this objection do not necessarily hold the second. Indeed, the second does not necessarily follow from the first. Hebert himself admits that the apostles could have had no successors in the sense of being eyewitnesses of the

Resurrection. He claims, however, that the apostolate meant more than this; they were the guardians of the faith. This is perfectly true, and in this sense the ministry has an apostolic function, but it is not creative as was that of the first apostles. As he admits, the "Apostolic Testimony is given in a permanent form in the New Testament."[20] The task of subsequent ministers is to safeguard it and to translate it into the idiom of their own day. This says nothing as to whether the ministry is to be that of presbyters or bishops. There is certainly no evidence in the history of the church these past three hundred years to prove that the faith has been better safeguarded by bishops than by presbyters.[21]

Hebert next turns to those who claim a presbyterial succession, rather than an episcopal one. As we have seen, the emergence of the single bishop in each church in the second century, or between the first and second centuries, is to some extent shrouded in darkness, and certainly the historical evidence does not permit his concluding words, "That which is of the *esse* of the Church is the essential core of the Ministry, namely the Apostolic Commission, *which the Bishop alone holds in its fulness, and is empowered to hand on* [italics mine]."[22] It is the italicized words which constitute a *non sequitur*, with the historical data available. The whole point is, What is the "essential

[ 178 ]

ministry" (as the Bishop of Oxford calls it)?[23]  Is it a ministry of bishops in regular succession?  Mere assertion does not prove it to be so.

Next, he deals with an important point raised by Daniel Jenkins, the point of the call of Paul to the apostolate.[24]  Here, it seems to me, he gives his case away, for he says:

> It is possible for this failure [forgetting the unseen King] to become habitual, and for the Church to become worldly; and then God will choose His own way to vindicate His honour, and will "work independently of His appointed ministers, or even against them," as He did when Jerusalem of old sinned against Him, and was visited with ruin and captivity.[25]

May we not claim with humility that this is exactly what God did do at the Reformation?  Again, what he says here has no relevancy for episcopacy as the *only* way in which the apostolic commission can be carried on in the church.

The fourth point deals with the high priesthood of Christ and the priesthood of *the church,* related to the claim that the "priesthood of all believers" means that ministering belongs to all "the 'saints' in general; the New Testament knows of no hierarchy."[26]  If "hierarchy" is taken in its strict etymological sense, it may be admitted that this claim is made by Protestants, but if it means simply an ordered ministry, then no major

Protestant church makes any such claim. Father Hebert admits that the emphasis on the priesthood of the church "expresses a positive truth of the first importance,"[27] and he is genuinely anxious throughout his book to bring the church, as distinct from the hierarchy, back into the picture. He recognizes the debased form of much Catholicism of the present day. But he does claim that the ministry is sacerdotal. On the other hand, Protestants, in arguing against sacerdotalism, often speak as though priesthood were done away in Christ. It is not less priesthood that we want, but more. The priestly nature of the church and of its office is everywhere asserted in the New Testament,[28] but is there a *sacerdotium in sacerdotio*? Canon Phythian-Adams says that there is no trace of it in the New Testament.[29] He goes on to say:

> There is but one Royal Priesthood in Biblical theology, and that is the Priesthood of Israel, predicted by the prophets and consummated in Christ, the new King-Priest of Zion after the order of Melchizedek. And as there is one Priesthood, so there is but one offering, the free-will offering of itself which the new Israel presents through Christ its Mercy Seat and Altar. And these two facts together preclude the possibility of a second "internal" priesthood. No man can offer himself except that man himself, no one can present some other person's love to God vicariously; and what is true of the individual is not less but far more true of Israel, whose offering is itself the very essence of its Priesthood.[30]

Whatever priesthood the ministry has is a *representative* priesthood. It cannot be sacerdotal in the true meaning of that word.

Point five has to do with the distinction between a charismatic and an official ministry, a distinction which has been familiar since the discovery of the *Didache*. Father Hebert rightly dismisses this distinction between form and spirit as an outrage.[31] He admits, however, that there is always grave danger of a form without the Holy Spirit and says that Catholics are always needing the warning spoken by Barth: "The true church is distinguished from the false only by the fact that in her Jesus Christ is *present in power*."[32] He quite rightly points out, however, that this need not, and does not, mean that structure is unimportant. To consider it unimportant is a grave weakness of much Protestantism.

The real crux of the matter is reached in his last point, where he discusses whether nonepiscopal ministries are real. Here he quite rightly deprecates the ambiguity of certain recent Anglican statements that nonepiscopal ministries are real but irregular. He asks whether these statements are to be taken to imply that nonepiscopal ministries mean the same thing as Anglican ministries. His own position is unequivocal. He says frankly, "They do not."[33] It is obvious that for him ministers not episcopally ordained are "laymen" and nothing more. He sees a hope of re-union by approaching the matter in this way and by inviting Methodist ministers to become leaders of religious societies within the church, and Presbyterian, Congregationalist, and Baptist ministers to become "lecturers" in parish churches! Well, it seems to me a faint hope and hardly likely to be realized. All through this discussion he has assumed "that the Apostolic Ministry, *as embodied in the office of Bishop,* is one of the essential forms of the Church [italics mine]"[34]—and that is the point which still remains to be proved.

An important matter is raised by Gregory Dix in his chapter on "Ministry in the Early Church" in *The Apostolic Ministry.* He claims that "the prayerful choice of a man by the 'Spirit bearing' Body of Christ is a choice by the Spirit" (p. 199).[35] He sees in the bishop the need for a twofold authorization, that of the people whom he represents and that of God.

> He is and must be the genuine choice of his own Church; only so can he stand for it before God to "propitiate His countenance," and before the world to proclaim the revelation of God with which his particular Church, the microcosm of "the" Church, is divinely charged. A multitude of passages can be cited which emphasize the extreme importance attached in Pre-Nicene times to the bishop's proper and free election. (P. 198.)

[ 182 ]

He points out that Catholic Christianity has failed to perpetuate this necessary element. In pre-Nicene times there was no such thing as "retired bishops, retaining the exercise of their orders without a see, no assistant bishops, no translations from see to see" (p. 199).[36] He claims: "It is thus the fourth-century Church order, not that of the first, second or third centuries, which has perpetuated itself in Catholic Christendom. That is different—in some respects very different—from what had preceded it, even though it is continuous with it" (p. 287). Finally, he makes the claim that in the pre-Nicene church, "A genuine election by his own Church and the free acceptance of him by all its members as their bishop (symbolized by the kiss of peace given to him by all immediately after his consecration) were as much a *sine qua non* for the episcopate as consecration" (p. 199).

If this is so—and I do not think that the matter has been put too strongly—then it would appear that there is no validly consecrated bishop in Christendom today. The point Gregory Dix raises is an important one, for it concerns the function of the church as such. He goes on to say:

> We should all be a long step nearer agreement if we recognized that the modern Protestant Societies [why not churches?] cannot be "given" or "asked to accept" *episkopē* in the ancient sense at all, because they already have it. It is

an inseparable accompaniment of any corporate Christian life, and the Protestant ministries have every right to be suspicious of our attempts to thrust a merely "Administrative" episcopate upon them, as casting doubts upon the reality of their own ministerial office. . . . All Reformed ministries alike were by intention what the *zeqenim* had been, public ministries to God with an ecclesiastical authority from a particular Society of Christians. As such they have a real pastoral office and authority, and a responsibility in and for the Society which has chosen and authorized them to guide its Christian life, to teach, to baptize, to celebrate the Lord's Supper, even—like the Jewish presbyteries—to "hand on the Spirit" by the laying on of hands to fill up their own number. All this is *episkopē*. And inasmuch as these ministries are the freely chosen organs of their own Societies to exercise it, they are in one respect better entitled to the style *episkopoi* in the ancient sense than the Anglican nominees of the State. (Pp. 295-96.)

He again refers to the free election by the church to the pre-Nicene bishop's office as being as much a *sine qua non* as was his consecration at the hands of other bishops.

Surely this all points to the fact that "the community, the church, the multitude of the faithful, are the fountain of official power. This power descends from the body itself—not from its servants. . . . The body of Christ, under him as its head, animated and led by his Spirit, is the fountain and spring of all official power and privilege. . . . The church is the mother of all the sons and priests of God."[37]   In this understanding of the matter, the original apostolate is something quite unique. We may grant that the apostle was the *shaliach* of the Lord, in the Jewish sense of full representation, sent forth and commissioned to represent the Lord. Even this, however, carried with it no guarantee of infallibility. There was a Judas among the apostles, and Paul himself was anxious lest he might become a castaway (1 Cor. 9:27). Did this apostolic authority descend upon the ministry of the church and particularly upon the bishop? Is there any evidence that a *shaliach* could appoint a *shaliach*, and that the *shaliach* so appointed, at the second remove, was conceived of as possessing in precisely the same way the same representative power of the original sender? I know of none. It is much more in keeping with the biblical doctrine of the church, with the *personal* emphasis of the whole Bible, with the conception of the church as "the fellowship of the beloved" and the body of Christ, that that which constitutes the apostolicity of the church is her faithfulness to the apostolic tradition, and that the power of choice and ordination is within her own life, as she commits herself to the Head of the church and to the guidance of his Spirit.

The fear is entertained that this would leave the ministry in the church powerless and ineffective, the slave of the people in the same way that a popularly elected political representative is subject to his constituency.[38] This is a genuine fear, and it points to a real danger. It arises from the fact that we are ever tempted to think of the church in worldly and political ways. But the church is something quite different. It is neither an autocracy nor a democracy so far as its earthly government is concerned. The relationships within the church are much nearer to those in a family, and the minister, whether presbyter or bishop, exercises authority much more in the way that a father does in a family.[39] Gregory Dix rightly claims that the minister requires double authorization, that of the free choice of the church in which he is to minister, and that of God as the minister of Christ. If election to office as presbyter or bishop is carried out as an act of worship, the church corporately giving herself to the guidance of God by his Spirit, then both these things are guaranteed. And if the ordination is similarly carried out, then it means, not only that the congregation transfers to him whom they have chosen certain rights, duties, and privileges, but also that by his ordination he becomes God's chosen minister to that congregation. Christ appoints his ministers, but he does so *through the church.*

The freedom of the ministry, in its preaching and pastoral office, within the bounds of the apostolic tradition, is a most important matter. Let us admit that it has often been grossly abused in nonepiscopal churches, especially in these latter years. But this abuse is no real part of the classical Protestant understanding of the ministerial office. Let me quote some words of the late Bernard Lord Manning, delivered at an ordination service in a Congregational church:

> The things that make a man a good minister of Jesus Christ come from God most high: you can neither bestow nor take them away. The weakness or the strength, the coldness or the devotion of the Church that ordains, as you ordain to-night, affect not in the least the validity or the fulness of the august commission that a minister receives. At your hands indeed he receives the commission; but it is Christ's commission, not yours; and it comes from Christ, not you. When your minister speaks mark whose word it is that he speaks. You do not hear from him an echo of your own voice. It is the Word of God that he proclaims, no word that you have committed to him to-night. The minister is not the creation of the Church. The Church is sometimes his creation.[40]

This is as fine a statement of the classical Protestant conception of the ministry as one could find, and it ought to go a long way in assuring Catholics that the Protestant churches have a sound doctrine of the ministry, even though they conceive of succession as being maintained *in the church* rather than *in the hierarchy* itself. The hierarchy is not a self-perpetuating entity *apart from the church.* That is why it is that to think of the apostolicity of the church as being maintained by episcopal succession is not possible for Protestants, however much they value historic continuity and the guarantee of it which an episcopal succession gives. They cannot set the church and the ministry apart in the way that the strict Catholic doctrine of apostolic succession demands. To do so would be to deny the nature of the church as revealed by the biblical and apostolic doctrine of the church. That church is apostolic in which the apostles' doctrine is preached and taught, in which the sacraments are administered with the unfailing intention of the apostles, who delivered them to us from the Lord, and in which this is safeguarded by a ministry, freely chosen by the church as it is guided by the Holy Spirit, and bearing the apostolic commission.

# EPILOGUE

If PROTESTANTS have been apt, in the nineteenth century and later, to divide between the gospel and the church, it is equally true that Catholics, since the fifth century, have tended to divide between the hierarchy and the church. Nevertheless, these past thirty years have seen a shifting of the emphasis in both cases to the recovery of *biblical* theology among both Catholic and Protestant scholars. This recovery of biblical theology has meant that Protestants have become more conscious of the origins of their witness in the classical Protestantism of the sixteenth century, and Catholics, in the same way, have become more conscious of the springs of their origin in the Patristic age of the first four centuries, before declension set in. The result has been to narrow the gulf which separates essential Catholicism from essential Protestantism. It is doubtful whether, on the doctrine of the church, anything like the chasm separates them which it was supposed existed. Protestants have seen quite clearly that neither the Bible nor classical Protestantism knows anything of Christianity without the church, while Catholics are beginning to realize the serious danger of substituting a "high-clericalism" for the "high-churchism" of the Bible and of Primitive Catholicism.

Naturally, this irenicon, which has proceeded from the vanguard of scholars in both fields, has met with resistance from the entrenched forces of the rear guards in both camps. Books and documents have appeared which can only be described as counterblasts. The present volume is not one of these counterblasts. It has been written, rather, with the aim of helping forward the work of understanding between Protestants and Catholics which is necessary to the emergence of that *una sancta*, which in our day is most desirable, not only because the Lord wills it, but because that without it the world can hardly be saved from perishing. Moreover, it is written by one whose whole life has been spent in a part of the Christian church which, well over a century ago, raised the standard of ecumenicity against the divisive tendencies which threatened the life of the body of Christ, and which has been described by Professor Will of Strassbourg as a "bridge church" between Protestantism and Catholicism (*Ministry and Sacraments*, p. 499).

It is now recognized on all sides that the solution of our difficulties will come from a realistic study of the Bible, and throughout I have attempted to let the Bible speak for itself. The newer understanding of what the Bible means by "revelation," as over against what our theologies and theories have made it mean, has contributed to the richer understanding of what the church is, in relation to the gospel and in relation to the Israel of God. In writing of "The Coming of the Church" and in dealing with "Jesus and the Church" and the doctrine of the church in Paul, the Johannine writings, and other documents of the New Testament, I have tried to elucidate these points. It is then that the nature of the church is revealed as a historical reality, as the instrument which is set in the world to achieve God's purpose of redemption, a redemption which penetrates into every area of life. On that point we are now mostly agreed, and this means that we recognize that the church, as God's gift to man, is an abiding reality with historical continuity; that it is *one* church in all ages and all places; that it is *catholic,* breaking the bounds, not only of time and place, but of class, race, and sex; and that it is, therefore, *apostolic,* one with the church of the apostles.

But how is this continuity maintained? It is here that we enter the realm where differences are still most acute, and in the last two chapters I have tried to make some contribution to their removal, and I hope not altogether failed. I have tried to show that neither indifference to questions of order and structure (often rightly, I think, ascribed to Protestant thought and practice), nor overzealous pleading for the acceptance of rigid, legal, and almost mechanical forms of structure (often, I am afraid, the attitude of Catholics), can get us very far, if any distance at all. From the Protestant side, we may not accept as true a doctrine which appears to be a contradiction of the very nature of the church, and of the gospel which reveals the church as part of the "good news" in Christ Jesus. The Catholic is equally concerned that we should not be indifferent to, nor set ourselves in opposition to, those forms of the church which it has pleased God in his wisdom to reveal to us. He should understand, however, that the real difficulty in accepting the rigid theory of apostolic succession, from the Protestant side, is not indifference to forms. It is something much deeper. If God is personal, and if he has chosen to deal *personally* with his children, being the Father of his family, it ill becomes us to attempt to hedge him in with *legal* restrictions, which would seem to be foreign to the way of his dealing with his children. Likewise, the Protestant should understand that the concern of the Catholic for form and structure in the church is dictated neither by his love of exclusiveness nor by a mere antiquarianism. It, also, is something much deeper. If God, in his personal dealing with man, reaches down to us in the limitations of our historical existence, in the Person of his Son, taking on the "form" of a servant, we cannot be wholly indifferent to the "form" which the church, the body of Christ, must take in history, setting spirit against matter and function against form in a way which is decidedly unbiblical. Understanding each other at this deeper level, we leave the area of controversy and enter that of conference, where partisanship and a sense of superiority are banished and only truth prevails.

The times are waxing late; our situation is extremely critical. But, there are signs of better things: the winds of God are blowing strong. In this year of our Lord, 1948, the Assembly of the World Council of Churches will meet to bring the Council into being. This, in the destiny of God, is a far more momentous event than the catastrophic upheaval of the recent world war, though few, if any, historians of our day will so record it, if they record it at all. In like manner, the secular historians of old treated the coming of our Lord, his life, his crucifixion, and his resurrection. Such a cavalier attitude need not disturb us whose confidence is in God. In the midst of the chaotic world situation in which we find ourselves, with its pessimism, its rival ideologies, its hatreds and brutalities, there stands one sure rock of refuge, the ancient gospel of our redemption in Christ Jesus; and one sure beacon shedding forth its light into the surrounding darkness, the church of the living God, against which the gates of Hades cannot, and do not, prevail.

> In vain the surge's angry shock,
>   In vain the drifting sand;
> Unharmed upon th' eternal Rock
>   Th' eternal City stands.

# APPENDIX A

## THE CHURCH IN THE EPISTLE TO THE HEBREWS

THIS document, like Melchizedek who appears in it, is without genealogy; we cannot say certainly who wrote it, to whom it was written, or from what place it originated. Among the Epistles of the New Testament, there are many ways in which it is unique. It does not begin as a letter, and yet it ends as one. It is the only document in the New Testament which has a definitely worked out *theory* of the atonement. In its reference to "shadow" and "substance" it is more influenced by Platonic thought than is any other New Testament document. It appears *at first sight* to be expressing Christianity in thought forms totally different from those of Paul and from those of any of the Gospels. It looks at Christianity through its worship forms more than any other document except the Apocalypse, but it has none of the characteristics of apocalyptic. Like the Apocalypse it is concerned with the heavenly priesthood of our Lord;[1] and yet no document, with the exception of the Fourth Gospel, is so realistic about his earthly life.[2]

[ 195 ]

In spite of its Platonism, however, the document is thoroughly Hebraic; and whatever else is dubious about it, it is certain that for the writer of the Epistle, the church is a reality, organized over against Jewry. It had been founded by apostolic-men, who had preached the word of God (13:7); it had its definite pastoral ministry endowed with *episcopē* (13:17-24); it cherished and safeguarded the apostolic tradition (2:1-4; 6:1-2); it possessed its own forms of worship, which is conceived of as priestly and sacrificial (10:19-25); and it practiced the Christian way of life (chap. 13). Christianity apart from the church is certainly unknown to the writer of this document, as it must have been to its recipients.

The book is dominated by the conception of the high priesthood of Christ (2:17-18; 4:14-16; 5:1-10; 6:20; 7:28; 9:11-14), which appears again in 1 Peter and in the Apocalypse. This priesthood is of a different order from that of Aaron. It is of the eternal order, a notion which is expressed by the introduction of the strange Old Testament figure, Melchizedek. It is carried on in heaven as well as upon earth. Priesthood is explained as "standing in with" weak, sinful, and needy humanity. The supreme act in history of this "standing in with" is the Incarnation. We are reminded of the words of Ezekiel in the Authorized Version, "I sat where they sat" (3:15).

Sacrifice is also of a different order from that of the Old Testament. It is *living* sacrifice, and it is *willing* obedience to the will of God. In the act of the once-for-all sacrifice on Calvary, Christ is both Priest and Victim; it is a true self-offering. Because of this high priesthood of Christ, the church is a priestly body, and worship is sacrificial (13:15). The church is continually engaged in offering herself in Christ, as being a partaker of Christ (3:14). This is the same intimate relationship between "the Christ" and "the church" that we have noted in Paul and in another form in the Johannine writer.

The relationship between the old Israel and the new Israel, which we have noted elsewhere, is maintained here, in spite of the writer's Platonism, which leads him to think of the Old Covenant as merely a shadow of the New. In spite of the contrast between the old Israel and the church, which is elaborated in chapters three and four, there can be no question that for him the church really extends backwards into the Old Testament. This is shown by his long list of saints and martyrs in chapter eleven, where he goes so far as to say that Moses "considered abuse suffered for the Christ greater wealth than the treasures of Egypt" (11:26; cf. 1 Cor., chap. 10). There is in this Epistle a clearer understanding of the oneness of the church in heaven and the church on earth than anywhere else except in the Apocalypse. In worship, heaven and earth intermingle; and in their life, Christians have already "tasted . . . the powers of the age to come" (6:5). The striking passage describing Christian worship, "But you have come to Mount Zion and to the city of the living God, the heavenly Jerusalem, and to innumerable angels in festal gathering, and to the assembly of the first-born who are enrolled in heaven, and to a judge who is God of all, and to the spirits of just men made perfect, and to Jesus, the mediator of a new covenant, and to the sprinkled blood that speaks more graciously than the blood of Abel" (12:22-24), shows that the Christians in worship stood in the heavenlies. This is the "realized eschatology," which is familiar in the rest of the New Testament, which was a feature of the first apostolic preaching, and which marked both the life and worship of early Christians.

The word *ecclēsia* appears but twice in the Epistle (2:12; 12:23). It is not a characteristic word of the writer. The term "body of Christ" does not appear at all. In this the author is like the Johannine writer. The curious phrase "the assembly of the first-born" (12:23) presents some difficulty. It may refer to the heroes of the past who have appeared in the previous chapter. On the other hand, the whole passage may be thinking of the future consummation as vividly realized in the present moment. In that case, "first-born" may refer simply to the baptized.[8] In different, but parallel, language the "first-born" are those who have passed through the "first death" and the "first resurrection." This would link the writer closely to the circle in which the writer of the Apocalypse moved.

If the writer does not use the expression "the body of Christ" and scarcely uses *ecclēsia*, he is rich in other expressions for the church. It is the house of God (3:6; 10:20), a familiar Old Testament expression for the temple; it is the people of the new covenant (8:7-13; 9:1, 15); it is the fellowship of "the saints" (9:10); it is Mount Zion (12:22), "the heavenly Jerusalem" (12:22), "the city of the living God" (12:22). In chapter eight the idea of the church as the "true tabernacle," which the Lord pitched, not man, is introduced, and Christ is the Minister of this true tabernacle (8:2). Here again is a linking point with the Apocalypse (Rev. 21:3) and with the prologue to the Fourth Gospel, where the word is hidden in our English translation (John 1:7). The idea, as expressed in the prologue to the Fourth Gospel, is that in Christ, God dwelt with men in all his fulness, the idea which Paul expresses in other language (Col. 1:19). In Hebrews and in the Apocalypse, this idea is expanded to the conception that in the church, God dwells with men and that there his full Presence is realized. Behind these passages there obviously lies the narrative in the twenty-third chapter of Exodus:

> Whenever Moses went out to the tent, the people would all rise and stand, each at the doorway of his tent, and gaze after Moses until he entered the tent; and as soon as Moses entered the tent, the column of cloud would descend, and stand at the doorway of the tent while he conversed with Moses; and whenever the people saw the column of cloud standing at the doorway of the tent, the people would all rise, and make obeisance, each at the doorway of his tent. The LORD used to speak to Moses *face to face, as one man would speak to another.**

What had been foreshadowed in Moses and the Old Testament had now been actually realized in the coming of Christ and the establishing of the church— God had actually dwelt with men in the Person of Christ and did now dwell with them in the fellowship of the church. Already the church on earth was in heaven. While here on earth, surrounded by tribulation, she awaits with patience the consummation of all things; but she already lives her life in the heavenlies and has "tasted . . . the powers of the age to come."

---

*\*The Bible: An American Translation,* by Smith and Goodspeed, Exod. 33:8-11. Used by permission of the University of Chicago Press.

## APPENDIX B

## THE CHURCH IN 1 PETER

HERE again, neither the word *ecclēsia* nor the term the "body of Christ" appears. Nevertheless, it is clear that for the writer the church is a real entity, definitely organized, with presbyters exercising *episcopē* (5:1-4). Not only so, but it is organized as over against the pagan state of Rome, from which it is already threatened with persecution and martyrdom; and in the eyes of the writer it has a significance which is far greater than that of the Roman State. He speaks of the church in the most exalted terms, while at the same time he is fully aware of what might be called its "ordinariness" and can apply to it a term no more exalted than that of "the brotherhood" (2:17). This is the true mystery of the church, and we have noted elsewhere in the New Testament that it is composed of such ordinary people, and to an outsider must have appeared as almost commonplace; while at the same time it has such outreaching ontological significance. Perhaps in no writing in the New Testament is this contrast so vividly portrayed as in 1 Peter.

This exalted character of the church is brought out at the very beginning by its being called "the elect" (1:2). The church is predestined in the foreknowledge of God in the same sense that the church has a destiny within history which is related to eternal reality, for the church is "the elect . . . according to the foreknowledge of God the Father" (1:1-2). Again, in chapter two, the church is "an elect race" (2:9). What is asserted of the church is asserted of the Christ, who was foreknown indeed "before the foundation of the world but was made manifest at the end of the times for your sake" (1:20). This shows the close identity of "the Christ" with "the church," which we have seen in Paul, and which later appears in the Johannine writer. This idea of the foreknowledge and "determinate counsel" of God was part of the primitive *kērygma* (Acts 2:23; 3:18).

The word used for "the elect" (*eklektos*) is the equivalent of the Hebrew *bachir*, found in Second Isaiah (42:1; 45:4; 65:9, 22) for God's chosen people, and is related to *ecclēsia* (the called-out people). It is evidently a technical word for the church and is so used by the Johannine writer (2 John, vs. 13) and by Paul (Rom. 8:33; Col. 3:12). It appears also in the Pastoral Epistles (1 Tim. 5:21; 2 Tim. 2:10; Titus 1:1). It may be argued that it reaches back into the teaching of Jesus, for it is used in the same

way in the Synoptic Gospels (Matt. 24:22, 24, 31;
Mark 13:20, 22, 27; Luke 18:7).[1] The idea and the
use of the word are therefore not new to Peter, but
whereas in other New Testament writers the idea is
never absent in relation to the church, in this Epistle
it is the dominant idea. One might almost say that
*eklektos* is a substitute for *ecclēsia*. The church is "an
elect race" (2:9), a new order of people transcending
the barriers of ordinary race and overlapping national
boundaries, having its foundation in heaven.[2] In this
sense it can hardly be doubted that, for the writer, the
church is the equivalent of the Kingdom of God, or
at least the spearhead of the kingdom. The actual
term "kingdom of God" does not appear in his letter.
In this notion of the church as "the chosen people of
God," a "holy people" (2:9; cf. 1:15), there is the
same close relationship between the "old Israel" and
the "new Israel" which we have noted in Paul. True,
a contrast is made between the old and the new, but
if there is contrast, there is continuity: "But you are
a chosen race, a royal priesthood, a holy nation, God's
own people, that you may declare the wonderful deeds
of him who called you out of darkness into his mar-
velous light. Once you were no people but now you
are God's people; once you had not received mercy
but now you have received mercy." Here at last the
"true Israel of God" has appeared. This Israel is

God's special possession, his *peculium,* his chosen, as Abraham, Isaac, and Jacob were his chosen ones. They are a "holy nation" (2:9) set in the world to work God's will and to reveal him to men. The church is unlike any other society, for it is the peculiar instrument of his eternal purpose. Further, while "in the world," Christians are not "of the world," as the Johannine writer later puts it. The same idea is expressed here by the phrase "aliens and exiles" (2:11).

The last of the exalted titles given to the church is that of the "royal priesthood" (2:9) or "holy priesthood" (2:5). The church thus fulfills the Messianic expectation of the coming King-Priest, which had already been fulfilled in the coming of her Lord. Here again we see the close identity of Christ and the church. The work which he accomplished, which in time was once for all, and which in eternity was full and complete, the church continues in the time process. Christians suffer with him (chap. 4); they are sharers of Christ's sufferings (4:13) and thus perform their priestly work. Likewise, they will be sharers of Christ's glory and thus achieve the kingly victory (4:13; 5:10).

The relationship between the church on earth and the church in heaven is implied rather than stated. That, for this writer, the church is a kingdom of two realms, heaven and earth, cannot be doubted. He even declares that the effects of Christ's redemption reach into Hades (3:19; 4:6) and thus backward into the time of the patriarchs. At any rate, the church is not to be measured by its earthly resources as they would appear to the outsider. A good deal of the Epistle may be regarded as springing from the necessity to make plain to catechumens who were seeking to enter the church the true nature of its being, its august reality in contrast to its seeming weakness in the face of the terrible might arrayed against it.[3] It is endowed with supernatural strength, "the strength which God supplies"(4:11).

# APPENDIX C

## THE CHURCH IN THE APOCALYPSE

IF HEBREWS is addressed to a situation of threatened persecution, and 1 Peter is to a situation in which persecution has already begun, the Apocalypse is addressed to a situation in which persecution is intense. Already the church has provided a noble roll of martyrs. It is now actually in a life-and-death struggle with pagan forces, represented in the might of Rome, styled as "Babylon the great, mother of harlots" (17:5; cf. 14:8; 16:19; 18:2, 10, 21) and said to be "drunk with the blood of the saints" (17:6). There can be no question here that the church is significant. In the first three chapters the word *ecclēsia* is used sixteen times in the singular or plural to refer to the local church and appears again, used in the same way, to refer to the local churches in 22:16. That the writer had just as firm a conception of the one church is revealed by the imagery of the book.

When stripped of the bizarre imagery common to apocalypses, the book reveals the same doctrine of the church that is found elsewhere in the New Testament.

Like Hebrews, 1 Peter, and the Johannine writer, the writer of this document does not use the Pauline term the "body of Christ," but he knows of nothing that is incompatible with it. As in Hebrews, there is a clear understanding of the relationship between the church in heaven and the church on earth. It might be said that in the Apocalypse this idea dominates all he has to say about the church (see 7:9-17; 14:1-5). The church is a transcendent reality. Its worship, which goes forward on earth, is the counterpart of the heavenly worship around the throne of God. Its suffering life is related to the sufferings of Christ, whose sacrifice is eternal in the heavens, for he was "the Lamb that was slain" "before the foundation of the world" (13:8).

There is, again, the mystery of the "ordinariness" of the church, with its seeming weakness and ineffectiveness, and its august majesty. It is still the fellowship of "our brethren" (12:10), men and women of humility and meekness; and yet it is the possessor of all might and power: "the kingdom of the world has become the kingdom of our Lord and of his Christ" (11:15). What is to be accomplished in the future has already appeared in the present. In the midst of bloody persecution, the seer can look forward to the consummation of all things and see "a great multitude which no man could number, from every nation, from all tribes and peoples and tongues, standing before the throne and before the Lamb, clothed in white robes, with palm branches in their hands, and crying out with a loud voice, 'Salvation belongs to our God who sits upon the throne, and to the Lamb!' " (7:9-10). And to him, this is a present reality. This is the real situation, however appearances may contradict it. The one solution against armed might and totalitarian rule is not "the Lion of the tribe of Judah," but the "Lamb standing, as though it had been slain," for the "Lion" of Judah and the "Lamb" slain "before the foundation of the world" are identified as one and the same (5:5-6).

The familiar expression "the saints" is used of the church (17:6; 19:8), which is also the "new Jerusalem, coming down out of heaven" (21:2). Here, too, as in Paul, the church is the bride of the Lamb (22:17). This idea is here elaborated, and the conception of the Bridal Feast of the Lamb, the Heavenly Banquet, is introduced (19:7-10). It is difficult to exclude from this idea the notion that the Eucharist is an anticipation of the Heavenly Banquet, a notion which has been expressed frequently in the hymns of the church. It was on "the Lord's day" that the writer was "in the Spirit" (1:10). Here "the Lord's day" may be taken to have a double reference; first to the day on which the weekly celebration of the Eucharist took place, and also to "the day of the Lord," the consummation of all things. *Sub specie aeternitatis* these two days are one. What the church does on earth is the antetype of what is consummated in heaven in the Lamb's Bridal Feast.

As in Hebrews, and as in the Fourth Gospel, we meet again with the idea of God as tabernacling with men:

> And I saw the holy city, new Jerusalem, coming down out of heaven from God, prepared as a bride adorned for her husband; and I heard a great voice from the throne saying, "Behold, the dwelling of God is with men. He will dwell with them, and they shall be his people, and God himself will be with them" (21:2-3).

Here, the holy city, the new Jerusalem, is the church, for it is identified with the bride of Christ. It may be argued that this has reference wholly to the consummation of all things, that the experience of God as tabernacling with men is an experience wholly in the future; but it would be hazardous so to argue. This writer, in true Semitic vein, plays fast and loose with tenses, especially with the present and the future. What is still to be, is already realized in the present. Already the *eschatos*, the end of history, has appeared in the midst of time. The cross, for this writer, is eternal in the heart of God. For him it is a past reality in history, already some sixty years behind him; it is also a reality yet to be experienced in the end of the ages, as it is being experienced now by the living church (5:1-14). The same is true of God's tabernacling with men. This writer would have agreed with the writer of the Fourth Gospel that in the historic Person, Jesus of Nazareth, God had tabernacled with men and that they had seen his glory (*shekinah*) (John 1:14). The place of this Presence was now the church, especially the church assembled for worship. Yet again, the completion of all that the Presence meant would be realized in the end of the ages.

Finally, as in 1 Peter, the church is a kingdom of priests; and Christians are "kings and priests unto God" (1:6; 5:10)[1] or "priests of God and of Christ" (20:6). The priestly and kingly nature of the church is indisputable in this writing. Its work on earth is priestly work, and its destiny is to sit with Christ upon his throne and reign with him: "Blessed and holy is he who shares in the first resurrection! Over such the second death has no power, but they shall be priests of God and of Christ, and they shall reign with him a thousand years" (20:6). The "first resurrection" and the "second death" are difficult expressions. Elsewhere I have given reasons for thinking that the "first resurrection" refers to baptism, by which the catechumen entered the church.[2] If this is so, the thousand

[ 211 ]

years' reign with Christ is going on at the time the book is being written. There is much in the book to indicate this.[3] In spite of all appearances to the contrary, the reign of the saints with Christ is actually proceeding at the moment, and the world is being judged. This is so, in spite of any futurist element in the Apocalypse. That which is still to come is already being realized. Such is the triumphant note of this book. And may we not say that history has justified its faith and hope!

# NOTES

## CHAPTER I

1. The words of Jesus in the Fourth Gospel have significance here: "No longer do I call you servants, for the servant does not know what his master is doing; but I have called you friends, for all that I have heard from my Father I have made known to you" (John 15:15).

2. See *Whither Theology?* Chap. 2. The question used to be discussed, Did Jesus ever found or intend to found a church? It still is discussed in books which, however modernistic, have an antiquated flavor. Reference was made to the fact that Jesus used the word "church" but twice (Matt. 16:18 and 18:17), and that these words were suspect as not being the words of Jesus but a piece of "church millinery." From my point of view, the argument is beside the point. Nevertheless, while the second of these passages evidently reports a word of Jesus in reference to the synagogue, adapted by the writer of the Gospel to refer to later church discipline, I have never been able to see why our Lord should not have used the word *ecclēsia*. It is everywhere used in the Septuagint, with which he was presumably acquainted, for the Hebrew word *qāhāl* (congregation), and must have been in common use in Galilee, where Greek culture was more widespread than in Judea.

3. See his *Cur Deus Homo* and his *Proslogion.*

4. "Abt Vogler," by Robert Browning, vii.

5. Robert Bridges, *The Testament of Beauty,* Book IV, line 1423.

6. I can best illustrate my meaning here by an analogy. I would assert that there is a mean between atomistic individualism as seen in the old liberalism, used in its doctrinaire sense, and the doctrine of the totalitarian state that the state is the superindividual. Both these attitudes are based on a failure to understand the nature of personality and on the confusion of "individual" and "person." Fellowship, which is the Christian gift to the world, transcends the contradiction between the individual and the whole. It is in the nature of a higher synthesis. And, as the Christian gift to the world, it is simply the revelation of the truth about reality.

7. From "Grace Divine," by Eliza Scudder.

8. See *The One and The Many in Israel's Conception of God,* by Aubrey Johnson.

9. Both Judaism and Christianity see Providence at work in history rather than in nature, and this means that the character of revelation is spiritual and moral and not theosophic. God is

THE BIBLICAL DOCTRINE OF THE CHURCH

not in nature as he is in persons and events. Nature is God's artistry, but man is made in the image of God, and he is made for fellowship with God. As J. Arthur Thomson said, "The universe consists of electrons, protons, radiation—and goodness"; and if this is so, revelation is given in the sphere of goodness. If this had been remembered we should have been spared certain doctrines of the church and of the sacraments, much too theosophic in character, which have appeared in the course of history.

10. The paradox of transcendence and immanence is possible only in a relationship in which one term is personal, and it is most perfectly possible in a relationship which is wholly personal.

11. It will be remembered that the Hebrew word is even used of sexual relationships, which goes to show how intimate the word was in meaning.

12. The Hebrew word *berith* (covenant) has nothing to do with a legal relationship, but with a warm-blooded personal relationship. It is a tragedy that it was translated in the Septuagint by the Greek word *diathēkē* (testament). It would better have been translated by *sunthēkē*. A century ago Alexander Campbell insisted on speaking of "The Old Covenant Scriptures" and "The New Covenant Scriptures," which is a more biblical way of speaking than to call them Old and New Testaments. Most modern scholars now agree.

13. From "Rugby Chapel," by Matthew Arnold. The true quality of sonship is to share the Father's innermost mind. See John 15:15, where the criterion of the friends of the Lord, as contrasted with servants, is that they have made known to them all things he has heard from his Father.

14. The reference is obviously to "the tent of meeting" (tabernacle) of Exod. 33:7-11 and "the glory of the Lord" (shekinah) associated with it, a reference which, along with the opening verses of the prologue, referring to Gen., chap. 1, show how Hebraic this part of the Fourth Gospel is.

15. Quoted by R. H. Lightfoot in *History and Interpretation in the Gospels*, p xiv.

16. *Christianity and the Nature of History*, by H. G. Wood, p. xxxviii.

17. It is often not realized how contradictory to the Greek notion of the foundation of ethics, and how offensive, this notion is. For the Greek, it was an impertinence to think that man could be an imitator of God, a matter refered to by the writer of the Epistle to Diognetus (*Cap.* X). It was, further, an impertinence to imagine that the gods were bound by the pettifogging regulations which were binding on men.

18. *The Bible To-day*, by C. H. Dodd, p. 157.

19. Hos. 2:14-20; Jer. 3:8; 2:2; Isa. 62:4, 5. See *The Bride of Christ*, by Claude Chavasse.

# NOTES

20. See Hos. 10:1; Jer. 6:9; Ezek., chap. 17.
21. Isa. 14:30; Jer. 23:3. The Hebrew words *sheerith* and *shear* obviously have a technical meaning in Isaiah, Jeremiah, Ezekiel, and in the postexilic prophets, Ezra, and Chronicles.
22. *The Coming of the Church*, by J. R. Coates; *The Teaching of Jesus*, by T. W. Manson.
23. *The Bible To-day*, by C. H. Dodd, p. 70.

## CHAPTER II

1. *The Rise of Christianity*, p. 267.
2. *Op. cit.*, p. 284. See also pp. 227-30.
3. See Harnack's *What Is Christianity?* and Loisy's reply, *The Gospel and the Church*.
4. It is one of the virtues of Alexander Campbell that he saw this corporate way of thinking as characteristic of the Bible, in a day when Protestant individualism was rampant, and consequently saw that there was no separation between gospel and church. See especially his essay on "The Body of Christ" in *The Christian System*. See further in the same volume his essays on "Foundation of Christian Union" and "Kingdom of Heaven." The same Catholic emphasis, as distinct from Protestant individualism, was, of course, present in Thomas Campbell's *Declaration and Address*, issued in 1809.
5. See a thorough and sober discussion of the question, Did Jesus found the church? in *The Historic Mission of Jesus*, by the late C. J. Cadoux, pp. 305-8. Here Dr. Cadoux also gives attention to that other kind of contention familiar in the Eschatological School of Johannes Weiss and Albert Schweitzer, that Jesus expected to return in glory within a comparatively short time and therefore could not have contemplated setting up a church. Dr. Cadoux, by the way, can hardly be conceived of as a scholar who "is bound to reach conclusions prescribed by the Christian communion to which he belongs"!

On the question of the apocalyptic background, it is interesting to have the comment of a Swedish scholar, Docent Olof Linton, in a recent book edited by Bishop Aulén, *En Bok om Kyrkan (A Book on the Church)*. Olof Linton contributes a chapter, *"Kyrka och ämbete i Nya Testamentet"* ("Church and Ministry in the New Testament") in which he says:

> It seemed that the newly discovered eschatology would definitely banish the ideas of Church and ministry from the world of the New Testament. If Christ expected the near approach of the End, He could not have founded a church; a man does not build a house on land that is in imminent danger of being flooded. No more could a Ministry transmitted by succession from one generation to another have lain within His horizon. So much seemed assured. Yet more thorough investigation has reversed this result. In the midst of the eschatological drama stands a figure with unique Divine

[ 215 ]

authority, the Messiah or Son of Man. But He does not stand alone; with Him is associated the Messianic Community, the new People of the new King, the new humanity of which the Son of Man is the first fruits. In this context of ideas the Church is an essential element; it is the new People of God, the new Israel. The Church is therefore not to be likened to a house built on land liable to flooding, but to a rock where those in danger can take refuge, over which the gates of death shall not prevail. (P. 102 [quoted by A. G. Hebert in *The Apostolic Ministry*, p. 495]).

6. See *Jesus and His Church*, by Dr. Newton Flew, pp. 52-58.
7. C. J. Cadoux, *The Historic Mission of Jesus*, p. 77.
8. *The Gospel and the Critics*, p. 15.
9. *Op cit.*, p. 335.
10. See the *Riddle of the New Testament*, by E. C. Hoskyns and F. N. Davey.
11. *The People and the Presense*, p. 143.
12. Rather, what St. Augustine did was to identify the kingdom, and hence the church, with a particular *political* entity, which was one of the most disastrous things he did do. The identification of kingdom and church need cause no surprise to those who are familiar with the writings of Alexander Campbell. See his essay on "The Kingdom of Heaven."
13. Matt. 9:35; 10:7; 11:12; 12:28; Mark 9:1; Luke 9:27; 11:20; 17:21.
14. Matt. 6:10; Luke 11:2; Matt. 13:24-30, 31-32, 33.
15. John 18:36. This is my only reference apart from that on p. 47 to the Fourth Gospel, but it will hardly be questioned than in this explicit statement before Pilate we have a summing up of what is implicit in the Synoptic teaching about the kingdom.
16. The fundamental mistake of the Western Church, after the time of Constantine, a mistake which reached through force of circumstances its logical conclusion in the Medieval Roman doctrine of the church as a political entity, was to identify too closely the church with the political order.
17. Cf. the description in the *Epistle to Diognetus* (*Cap.* V): "Every foreign land is to them a native country, and every land of their birth as a land of strangers."
18. See *The Apology of Aristides* (c. A.D. 135): "The world standeth because of Christians." This was an idea prevalent in the prophetic interpretation of the "old Israel."
19. For a fuller working out of these ideas, see *Whither Theology?* Chap. 3.

## CHAPTER III

1. *The Meaning of Paul for To-day*, by C. H. Dodd, p. 18.
2. See Bousset, *Kyrios Christos*, and Reitzenstein, *Poimandres*. For a modern examination of this problem, see Wilfred L. Knox, *St. Paul and the Church of the Gentiles*.

3. A similar realism was seen in the work of Alexander Campbell more than two generations earlier. See *The Christian System,* essays on "Baptism," "The Body of Christ," "Foundation of Christian Union," and "Remission of Sins."

4. See *Jesus or Paul?* by Arnold Meyer, published in English, 1909.

5. *Paul and Jesus,* published in English at the same time as Meyer's book.

6. See, for example, *Jesus and Paul,* by B. W. Bacon, first delivered as a series of Hibbert Lectures in 1920.

7. Contrast with this "The Place of the Sacraments in the Teaching of St. Paul," by Prof. Andrews, which in 1917 was included in P. T. Forsyth's book, *The Church and the Sacraments.*

8. See the exhaustive study of this question in, *"The Beginnings of Christianity,* by Lake and Foakes-Jackson and especially the work of Henry J. Casbury in those volumes. See also C. H. Dodd, *The Apostolic Preaching and Its Developments.*

9. *Contemporary Review,* July, 1941.

10. This was the view advocated by P. T. Forsyth in *The Church and the Sacraments,* p. 58: "The local Church was a community which was not self-contained, but which included spiritually all Christians everywhere. . . . The local Church was but the out-crop there of the total and continuous Church, one everywhere."

11. Another merit of Alexander Campbell was that he rejected the notion of "the invisible church," which had been advanced by Luther and by Calvin in a slightly different form. His stress on the *visible* church was another of his Catholic emphases.

12. This is true of all the Pauline Epistles, which are intimate *letters* and not formal epistles, with the possible exception of Ephesians, which I take to be Pauline though not necessarily written to Ephesus. I have refrained from using the Pastoral Epistles because the argument needs no support from them. Most scholars think of them as Pauline in substance but written by a later hand.

13. See Rom. 12:13; 16:15; 1 Cor. 16:1; 2 Cor. 9:12; 13:13; Eph. 1:1, 15; Col. 1:12, 26.

14. This practice is certainly later than the time of Augustine. It is parallel to another declension in an individualistic direction, which came in after the fifth century, but was threatening from the inception of monasticism. This was the practice of applying the idea of the church as the bride of Christ to individual monks and nuns. See *The Bride of Christ,* by Claude Chavasse. Both these declensions have their beginnings in Catholicism and have already done their work when Protestantism emerges. The irony is that the individualism which Catholicism deplores in Protestantism has its roots in Catholicism.

[ 217 ]

15. This was the prevailing Gnostic teaching which tended to ignore history. It is possible that as early as the Corinthian correspondence it had already begun to be a nuisance alongside other troubles in the Corinthian church. See two articles on "Gnosticism and Life" which I contributed to the *Expositor*, March and April, 1925.

16. This probably has reference to the introduction of converts to the prayer life of the church in the saying of the "Our Father" at the Eucharist. This was a well-established practice in the late second century.

17. This, in one sense, is the burden of Deuteronomy.

18. See Isa. 3:14; 5:7; Jer. 12:10. Cf. the Parable of the Vineyard, Luke 13:6-9.

19. See John, chap. 15. Cf. the Eucharistic prayer in the *Didache* for the "Holy Vine of David, Thy servant, which Thou didst make known through Jesus, Thy Servant."

20. See Ezek., chap. 37, which is a vision of the "new Israel" or resurrected Israel.

21. It dominates the thought of the Apocalypse. See text, pp. 207ff.

22. This is reflected in the Apocalypse. See text, pp. 209f.

23. Moffatt's translation. Cf. Eph. 2:6. It must be remembered that Philippi had only recently received colonial status and was now literally a piece of old Rome planted down in Philippi.

## CHAPTER IV

1. *The Johannine Epistles,* xlviii. Moffatt New Testament Commentary series.

2. Even Heiler, in his book, *Der Katholizismus,* pp. 66-76, sees only an *ecclesia invisibilis;* and Schlatter, in his *Die Theologie der Apostel,* p. 233, denies that there is any *visible* church in the Fourth Gospel. But Ignatius, a decade after the writing of this Gospel, while he uses *ecclēsia,* does not refer to the church as "the body of Christ." Nevertheless it would be absurd to conclude that he did not think of it as the body of Christ. It is possible that the expression "the body of Christ" had come to have a peculiar Docetic or theosophic meaning ascribed to it by this time. We know from the parallel of theosophy and anthroposophy in our own day how quite innocent expressions can be filled with a similar fantastic content and made dangerous to use. If this were so concerning the expression "the body of Christ," it would explain its absence from the Johannine writings and the Ignatian epistles. It is important to note that the phrase "my body" in connection with the Eucharist is discarded in the Fourth Gospel and "my flesh" used instead, an expression less capable of being given a Docetic twist.

3. *The Fourth Gospel: Its Purpose and Theology,* pp. 104-44.

[ 218 ]

4. The general tendency of nineteenth century criticism was in this direction from Strauss to Holtzmann and Loisy. See Holtzmann's *Johanneisches Evangelium* (1893) and Loisy's massive Commentary (1903). The tendency of all recent criticism has been against this position. See W. F. Howard's *The Fourth Gospel in Recent Criticism and Interpretation* (1931); *History and Interpretation in the Gospels,* by R. H. Lightfoot (1935); Sir Edwyn Hoskyn's Commentary; and the I.C.C., by J. H. Bernard.

5. *The Fourth Evangelist: Dramatist or Historian?*

6. See Hoskyn's note on this in his Commentary, pp. 152-64.

7. See Charles's volumes, *Apocrypha and Pseud-epigrapha;* see also H. H. Rowley, *The Relevance of Apocalyptic.*

8. See pp. 68f. Here the word *naos* is used.

9. John 5:1-18. Cf. the healing of the paralytic in Mark 2:3-12.

10. A constant note of the world's contempt for the church is that it is composed mostly of people of no account. It was uttered by Aelius Aristides, a friend of Marcus Aurelius, and later by Celsus. This, according to the Synoptics, to Paul, and to the Johannine writer, is the glory of the church.

11. Cf. Matt. 13:17; Luke 10:24; Heb. 11:13; 1 Pet. 1:10-12.

12. Heb. 13:20, "Our Lord Jesus, the great shepherd of the sheep"; 1 Peter 2:25, "The Shepherd and Guardian of your souls"; 5:4, "When the chief Shepherd is manifested."

13. This identity is found even in Homer. It is fairly common to pastoral peoples.

14. See Psalm 72, the Psalm of "The Ideal King," whose qualities are as much pastoral as judicial.

15. *The Natural and the Supernatural.*

16. An echo of the "one shepherd" of Ezek. 37:24.

17. The matter is again introduced in the addendum to the Gospel of John in the commission given to Peter to feed the Lord's sheep.

18. The same emphasis is made in the First Epistle.

19. This is the same temptation which came to Jesus at his Transfiguration, the temptation to escape the cross. At least this would seem to be implied in Luke 9:28-36.

20. Cf. Heb. 3:1, where Jesus is called "the apostle and high priest of our confession."

21. C. H. Dodd, *The Johannine Epistles,* p. 140. Moffatt New Testament Commentary series.

22. *Ibid.*

## CHAPTER V

1. Early Christians believed that the world would go to pieces if the church were taken out of it. See *The Apology of Aristides,* Cambridge Texts and Studies, Vol. I, pp. 50-51. And surely this is true, as for them, so for us.

2. This is the true mark of the apostolicity of the church. In all movements of God in history, there is always the quality of sentness about his witness. His servants go, but they are sent. It is not the impulse of desire, born within and reaching upward, but the objective compulsion of a sentness which characterizes all their action and words.

3. See Toynbee's massive volumes, *A Study of History.*

4. See Phil. 3:20; also Eph. 2:6 and Col. 3:1. The passage in Philippians presents some difficulty to the translator, but there is evidence that *politeuma* was in use to mean "a corporate body of citizens resident in a foreign country," equivalent to the Latin *colonia;* and Philippi had recently been made a colony. See *Orientis Graeci Inscriptiones Selectae,* 592 (ed. by W. Dittenberger); also *Corpus Inscriptionum Graecarum* (ed. by A. Boeckh) for such usage.

5. The word "fallible" is here used in relationship to our Lord to indicate that he "grew in wisdom," that there were things he did not know. It is not intended to mean that he was liable to err in the pronouncements which he made. The parallel here between our Lord and the church is not strictly accurate; the church is his creation, and he is the Head of the church, and as the Head and Creator, in him "dwells all the fulness of the Godhead." Nevertheless, in his incarnate state, he was "made in all points like as we, yet without sin," which involved limitation of knowledge, though this is restricted to those realms in which he was not specifically fulfilling his Messianic vocation.

6. What I say here does not apply to the Eastern Orthodox. Their doctrine of infallibility is generally misunderstood. The decree of any council is not binding upon the faithful until it has received confirmation in the life and witness of the church. There is an absence of logical and legal conceptions such as those which dominate the minds of Western Catholics. The Council of Florence (1439), which accepted papal supremacy, is an example of this. It became a "dead letter" although only one bishop had dissented. It is further illustrated by a letter issued in 1935 by an Orthodox priest on his condemnation by the Metropolitan Sergius: "The fact of the condemnation of my doctrine, . . . without any general discussion in the church, is not in keeping with Orthodox *sobornost,* and bears rather the character of Roman Catholic pretense to hierarchical infallibility, *ex esse,* in matters of faith."

7. A phrase I owe to Henry Nelson Wieman. See his *Wrestle of Religion with Truth.*

8. *Struggles and Triumphs of the Truth,* by Prof. J. W. Lowber, D.Sc., Ph.D., pp. 170-71.

9. Acts 19:32, 39, 41, where the word has reference to the assembly which objected to Paul at Ephesus.

10. This is the only sense in which the claim for diversity as over against uniformity in Canon Streeter's rather fanciful book, *The Primitive Church,* can be justified. It has not been sufficiently recognized that the book is at many points intended to be provocative and does not maintain the same level of seriousness throughout. This autonomy of the local church is maintained right down to the fifth century. Each local church centered in such areas as Jerusalem, Antioch, Caesarea, Ephesus, Rome, etc., had its own baptismal creed and its own way of celebrating the Eucharist, though baptism was baptism, the Eucharist was the Eucharist and not some ghostly shadow of it, and the creed expressed the one faith.

11. See the wise words of Alexander Campbell in *The Christian System,* Chap. XXIV.

12. This was the mistake made by the medieval church and continued by the modern Roman Church. The modern Roman Church, it must never be forgotten, is two things—a church and a political entity.

13. The church identified with a political party would be even more corrupt than the church identified with a political entity such as the state. The church herself cannot be concerned with political expediency. The political influence she exercises as the church must be from without and not from within any political party.

14. This was the great temptation which befell the Reformed churches in the sixteenth century. The Reformation itself did not create nationalism. The spirit of nationalism had already appeared in the fifteenth century and it was ready at hand when the Reformation began. The Reformation was made more possible because of it and, on the other hand, helped to foster it; but it did not create it. The Reformers themselves, being children of the Middle Ages, had no other conception than that status in a nation meant status in the church of that nation. Hence, once the church had been divided, it was natural to think of church and nation in the principalities of Germany and the cantons of Switzerland as being coterminous. In Lutheranism the result tended to be Erastianism; in Calvinism, "the rule of the saints." So far as the English scene is concerned, it was much more complex; hence the richness of free-church life there.

15. This is particularly true where free churches have so far forgotten their history as to be unaccustomed to an attitude which sets them against the government, and where church establishment is not of an Erastian kind. Recent history has shown us that the legal question of established versus free church is a minor one compared with the deep problem of God versus Caesar.

16. See *The Meaning of History,* by Nicholas Berdyaev, Chap. X.

17. In much of what I have written on church and state, I have been dependent on two articles I contributed to the *Hibbert Journal*, April, 1941, and April, 1943.

18. *Julius Caesar*, Act. IV, Scene iii, 217.

19. Without the recognition of this fact, Prof. Nygren reminds us, "the price to be paid for maintaining the purity of the idea of *agapē* might have been complete ineffectiveness." See his *Agapē and Eros*, p. 182.

### CHAPTER VI

1. By "theology" I mean the content of the word of God, and by "Christian theology" I mean the content of the word of God as given in the historic revelation of Jesus Christ as the Word of God made flesh—the holy energy of God, rather than the theosophic notion of God.

2. I can best show what I mean here by quoting some words of James Russell Lowell, which, though they are written about human giving, can reveal my meaning for the very reason that what can be said about human giving is valid, though not adequate, precisely because human giving is a reflection of the nature and character of divine giving. In one sense, the whole story of redemption can be summed up in the phrase "God gave," expanded to "God gave himself." Nothing less than this is ever adequate to the creation of fellowship. Here, then, are Lowell's words quoted from "The Vision of Sir Launfal":

> Not what we give, but what we share,
> For the gift without the giver is bare;
> Who gives himself with his alms feeds three,
> Himself, his hungry neighbor, and Me.

3. This is the burden of John Oman's book, *Grace and Personality*.

4. *Idem*, p. 22.

5. *Eudemian Ethics*, 1238*b*; quoted by James Moffatt, *Love in the New Testament*, p. 9.

6. *The Philosophy of Loyalty*, p. 15. See further on this point the first part of an article I contributed to the *Christian Union Quarterly*, July, 1929.

7. Schweitzer's accusation, in his *The Quest of the Historical Jesus*, that liberal Protestants had looked down a deep well, seen themselves reflected, and exclaimed, "Jesus!" will be remembered.

8. See *The Modernist Movement in the Roman Church*, by Alec R. Vidler.

9. See Thomas Campbell's *Declaration and Address*. Alexander Campbell constantly claimed that he had no *private* interpretation of his own of the Scriptures and appealed to the qualified and sanctified scholarship of the great doctors of the church, but

of the *whole* church. His treatment of baptism is an example of this, where he minutely examines the early Fathers and later teachers.

10. This is what came near to happening in the life of the Roman Catholic Church in the apologia presented for Catholicism by Loisy and Tyrrell. It actually happened in the gnostic churches of the conciliar period.

11. Alexander Campbell could say, "It is not the will of Jesus Christ, because it is not adapted to human nature, nor to the present state of his kingdom as administered in his absence, that the church should be governed by a *written* document alone" (*The Christian System,* p. 173).

12. From "Two in the Campagna," by Robert Browning.

13. In the case of a local church, this would mean literally the whole church. In the case of the church of an area, it would mean the churches by their representatives, but representatives of every order and not just the hierarchy. In the third century, and much later in some places, it was still customary for the *whole* church to express its voice, for instance in the election of the bishop.

14. This is what our Lord meant when he said in a moment of exaltation, "I thank thee, Father, Lord of heaven and earth, that thou hast hidden these things from the wise and understanding and revealed them to babes; yea, Father, for such was thy gracious will" (Luke 10:21). What we have to guard against is being wise in our own conceits and confident in our ignorance. Somewhere the mean has to be struck between dependence and independence, and it is only in fellowship—in a truly personal relationship, a worship act, which consists of giving, and receiving—that the mean can be struck; for in a truly personal relationship "we are nothing except what we receive, and yet we can receive nothing to profit except as our own," for then we receive without embarrassment.

15. The temper which Browning condemned in "Bishop Blougram's Apology" was this:

> The common problem, yours, mine, every one's,
> Is—not to fancy what were fair in life
> Provided it could be,—but, finding first
> What may be. then find how to make it fair
> Up to our means: a very different thing!
> No abstract intellectual plan of life
> Quite irrespective of life's plainest laws.

16. Since the work of the *Formgeschichte* school, it is no longer possible to neglect the Fourth Gospel. The gulf between the Fourth Gospel and the Gospel of Mark is now seen not to be so wide as was once supposed. Indeed, there is great similarity between the two Gospels. See what is said in Chapter IV; see

also *Die Formgeschichte des Evangeliums,* by Martin Dibelius. We have been driven to ask the question: Does the objectivity of history lie in fact without interpretation, as Ranke supposed in the early part of the nineteenth century? Can there be facts without meaning? If not, must we not with Quintilian still regard history in some measure as *proxima poetis et quondam modo carmen solutum?* (*Institutio Oratoria,* X, I, 31). After a somewhat arid spell of prosaic objectivity, which doubtless has brought its own gains, we are coming to see the truth of Walter Savage Landor's words, written as long ago as 1836: "History, when she has lost her Muse, will lose her dignity, her occupation, her character, her name" (*Pericles and Aspasia,* cxli). The *Formgeschichte* school has done much to deepen our understanding at this point.

17. See footnote, p. 114, in my book, *Christianity Is Pacifism.*

18. *Greek Philosophy,* Part I, p. 1, by John Burnet.

19. T. W. Manson suggests that there is a mistranslation of Aramaic here and that Jesus is only stating a fact and not the purpose of his teaching in parables. See *The Teaching of Jesus,* pp. 75ff. He is supported by C. C. Torrey, *Our Translated Gospels.*

20. A phrase which I owe to Alexander Campbell.

21. This is the burden of George Eliot's *Romola,* as it is of Browning's "The Grammarian's Funeral." We shall never understand the practice of self-discipline in the history of the church, unless we understand the large part played by the influence of this motive.

## CHAPTER VII

1. Luther's doctrine of "the invisible church," which later was halfheartedly adopted by Calvin, was a necessity of the times. It was "legislation for a particular instance," which is rarely a happy expedient. For him, it was necessary as a defense against the "great church" which had cast him out. Later, it became easy to read it back into the New Testament. Thus it became a normal Protestant doctrine. In the sense in which he propounded it, it is no part of the New Testament. Disciples of Christ may be glad that this was one of the elements of Protestantism which their early teachers vehemently rejected.

2. For this reason Christianity cannot be adequately expressed in terms of a metaphysic which is either idealist or realist, but only in terms of one which is idealist-realist.

3. We remember the picture which so influenced Luther in his decision to become a monk—the picture of a ship full of clergy, with the laity struggling in the water and catching at ropes idly thrown to them by the priests.

## NOTES

4. This is what should have happened down the ages. The special witness of each type of Christianity which has had permanence may be taken to be a real witness, and this witness should have been made possible in the "great church," as indeed it often was in the Middle Ages. The fault was not always on one side, but sometimes on one, sometimes on the other, and sometimes on both.

5. Edited by Kenneth E. Kirk. See, e.g., pp. 119-42, 228-32.

6. *The Nature of Catholicity,* pp. 112, 122.

7. I have discussed this in *Essays on Christian Unity,* Chap. V.

8. The ground has been shifted somewhat in *The Apostolic Ministry,* where everything seems to depend on *episcopē,* rather than upon *episcopos.* Attention will be given to this in the final chapter.

9. I have examined the evidence for this in *Essays on Christian Unity,* Chap. V.

10. *Dissertations on the Apostolic Age,* pp. 160ff.

11. *The Apostolic Ministry,* pp. 253-63.

12. *To the Trallians,* II and III.

13. *Against Heresies,* III, 3.

14. But see *contra* what is said by Beatrice M. Hamilton in *The Apostolic Ministry,* pp. 389-460, where it is argued that presbyterial ordination was allowed only in cases where no bishop was available. This may well be, but it by no means gets over the difficulty that it was allowed, and that such orders were regarded as valid. What would have happened in the case of baptism where there had been no opportunity for baptism? Would the Anglican Church have insisted on baptism? There can hardly be any question that it would. Why then not insist on episcopal ordination as it is doing today in reunion schemes, as, e.g., in Canada?

15. Book III, Chap. XXXIX.

16. The quotation is taken from Spottiswoode's account. See *History of the Church of Scotland,* Book VII.

17. Aquinas says: *"Sed episcopalis potest dependet a sacerdotali; qui nullus potest recipere episcopalem potestatem nisi prius habeat sacerdotalem. Ergo episcopatus non est ordo."* Billot, the Jesuit, says: *"Non est similis ratio de conseecratione episcopali quae omino nulla esset, si non pre-existeret character sacerdotalis; episcopatus enim non est ordo distinctus a sacerdotio ut jam doctum est, et infra ex professo declarabitur"* (*De Ecclesiae Sacramentis,* p. 268). Miss Hamilton, in *The Apostolic Ministry,* inclines to the view that the consecrations took part on the grounds of ordination *per saltum* and regards such a course as a "questionable procedure," pp. 416-21.

18. See *The Gathered Community,* by Robert C. Walton; and *The Fellowship of Believers,* by E. A. Payne.

## CHAPTER VIII

1. Baptism is not involved, for even lay baptism is allowed *in extremis* in the Western Church.

2. The Roman Church is the most rigid and denies the validity of Anglican orders, not only on the ground that the succession was broken at the Reformation (on the Roman view), but also on the ground of lack of intention in the rite of ordination. Rome does not deny the validity of Eastern Orthodox orders. Some Anglo-Catholics are as rigid as Rome, but by no means all.

3. There are certain safeguards which provide that no non-episcopally ordained minister will be forced on a congregation of the United Church, formerly of the Episcopal Church of South India, without its consent.

4. *Church and State*, p. 57.

5. *The Form of the Church*, p. 106.

6. *Idem*, p. 108.

7. *Ibid.*

8. *Idem*, p. 107.

9. *Ibid.*

10. *The Apostolic Ministry*, p. 202.

11. *The Form of the Church*, p. 109.

12. *Idem*, p. 113. The language here is loose because when the single bishop arose in the single church, he appears to have been the minister of baptisms and of the Eucharist. It is not until about the third century that the celebration of the Eucharist is delegated to presbyters. As to the ministry of the word, there is no evidence that the bishop was the sole minister, not even in the second century.

13. *The Way of At-one-ment*, p. 110.

14. *Idem*, p. 112.

15. *Didascalia, Cap.* XI.

16. Tertullian, *De Exhortatione Castitatis*, 7.

17. *The Way of At-one-ment*, p. 84.

18. An interesting and revealing commentary on the fact that lay celebration, if not unruly, was regarded as valid, is provided by the classical Catholic teaching that it is Christ himself who is the proper Minister of the sacraments (see St. Thomas Aquinas, *Sum. Theol.*, ques. 64, ans. 9), and by the fairly common practice of lay absolution in the Middle Ages (see *La Confession aux laiques dans l'église latine depuis le VIIIe jusqu' au XIVe siècle*, by A. Teetaert, 1926). Albert the Great defended it on the same grounds as lay baptism. The fact that down to the close of the tenth century it was common for laymen, including women, to act as ministers of *viaticum* is a further testimony to the thesis that originally what distinguished the laic from the cleric was not some *character indelibilis*, possessed by the latter and not by the former, the lack of which in the laic prevented him under any

circumstances from administering the Eucharist. This conclusion is further strengthened when we remember that John Teutonicus claimed that a layman, if need be, could perform the sacrament of confirmation (see Fr. Gillmann, *Die Lehre der Scholastik vom Spender der Firmung und des Weihesakramentes*, 1920). The strict Roman Catholic doctrine of the minister of the sacraments is that Christ our Lord is *minister principalis, primarius*, and that priests are only *ministri secundarii et instrumenttales*. In the 10th Canon of Session VII of the Council of Trent, an effort is made (though elsewhere it is admitted that baptism and matrimony may in certain circumstances be administered by anybody) to rebut Luther's claim that, under certain circumstances, a valid Eucharist might be celebrated by a layman. This had reference to the bull *Exsurge Domine* of the 15th of June, 1525. The bull itself is unconvincing, when it is remembered that the *pure* Roman doctrine admits that priests in their celebration are only subordinate servants, and when the Petrine declaration that we are all kings and priests unto God (1 Pet. 2:5) has to be explained away as purely figurative!

19. This view is also set forth in *The Apostolic Ministry*, pp. 184-303.

20. *The Form of the Church*, p. 111.

21. See *Essays on Christian Unity*, Chap. V.

22. *The Form of the Church*, p. 113.

23. See *The Apostolic Ministry*, pp. 3-52.

24. See *The Nature of Catholicity*, pp. 25-26.

25. *The Form of the Church*, pp. 113-14.

26. *Idem*, p. 110.

27. *Idem*, p. 116.

28. See Rom. 12:1; Phil. 4:18; Heb. 13:15; 1 Pet. 2:5, 9; Rev. 1:6; 5:10.

29. *The Way of At-one-ment*, p. 74.

30. *Idem*, pp. 75-76.

31. *The Form of the Church*, p. 117.

32. *The Knowledge of God and the Service of God*, p. 171.

33. *The Form of the Church*, p. 120.

34. *Idem*, p. 121.

35. See Chap. VI of this book, where the same point is made.

36. "The first known instance of translation is that of Alexander of Cappadocia to Jerusalem, noted as something exceptional and justified only by a miraculous vision" (Eusebius, *Eccles. Hist.*, VI, xi, 2).

37. Alexander Campbell, *The Christian System*, p. 84.

38. Alexander Campbell was well aware of this danger, as is revealed by the following words: "Before any community, civil or religious, is organized, every man has equal rights to do what seemeth good in his own eyes. But when organized, and persons appointed to office, then whatever rights, duties or privileges are

conferred on particular persons, cannot of right belong to those who have transferred them; any more than a person cannot both give and keep the same thing." (*Op. cit.*, p. 81.)

39. Campbell, on this head, arguing with those who rejected a ministry in the church, says: "But we shall be asked, 'Is not preaching, and baptizing, and even teaching, the common privilege of all disciples, as they have opportunity?' And we ask in answer, 'Is it not the privilege of all fathers to teach their own children, and to preside over their own families?'" (*Ibid.*)

40. *A Layman in the Ministry*, p. 153.

### APPENDIX A

1. See *The Ascension and Heavenly Priesthood of Our Lord*, by William Milligan.

2. See Chaps. IV and V of this book.

3. See an article on "The First Resurrection and the Second Death," which I contributed to *Theology*, May, 1943.

### APPENDIX B

1. These passages, except the last, are from the apocalyptic sections of the Gospels. With regard to Mark 13:14-20, Dr. C. J. Cadoux says that "it contains very little that Jesus himself could not have spoken" (*The Historic Mission of Jesus*, p. 276).

2. Cf. the second century apologists who argue that the church is a "third kingdom," coming after the Jewish and pagan kingdoms. See especially *The Apology of Aristides*.

3. Chap. 3, vs. 13, through chap. 4, vs. 11, may even be an address delivered to catechumens at their baptism. Many other parts of the Epistle appear to belong to a primitive Christian catechism.

### APPENDIX C

1. The A. V. is perhaps still the better translation of this passage. Cf. *The New Testament in English*, a new translation of the Vulgate issued by the Roman Catholic hierarchy in England, where 1:6 is translated, "and made us a royal race of priests, to serve God."

2. See an article of mine on "The First Resurrection and the Second Death" in *Theology*, May, 1943.

3. See 5:10, where it is said that the "royal race of priests" reign upon the earth. We must remember, too, that the kingdom and the church are identified in this book. This idea of "the rule of the saints" goes back to Daniel, a book which undoubtedly influenced the writer. In Daniel, the kingdom is assigned to the Son of man, and the Son of man is equated with "the saints of the most High" (see Daniel 7:13-27, A.V.).

[ 228 ]

# INDEX OF SUBJECTS

# INDEX OF NAMES